Indian Wars in North
1663-1763

D0932308

E. Lawrence Lee

Raleigh
Division of Archives and History
North Carolina Department of Archives and History

To Larry and James

CONTENTS

FOREWORD

Indian Wars in North Carolina, 1663-1763, by Lawrence Lee, was first published in 1963 by the Carolina Charter Tercentenary Commission and was reprinted in 1968 by the State Department (now North Carolina Division) of Archives and History. Long out of print, it now returns to the list of distinguished publications offered by this agency.

Enoch Lawrence Lee Jr. was born in Wilmington on New Year's Day in 1912. Even as a child he exhibited a keen interest in the history of the Cape Fear region. Such interest was perhaps inevitable, inasmuch as he was the grandson of Maj. James Reilly, the Confederate officer whose duty it was to surrender Fort Fisher to Union forces in 1865. In childhood, moreover, Lee counted the venerable James Sprunt, the patriarch of Cape Fear historians, as a friend. Entering college during the depression years, Lee obtained a degree in commerce from the University of North Carolina in 1934 and was employed by the New York firm of Arthur Andersen and Company as a certified public accountant. After serving in the U.S. Army during World War II, he made the career decision to become a professional historian. He returned to Chapel Hill, where his graduate work, directed by Prof. High T. Lefler, led to a Ph.D. degree in 1955. Lee's dissertation was subsequently published with minor revisions as *The Lower Cape Fear in Colonial Days* (1965). Among his other published works were *New Hanover County: A Brief History* (1971) and *The History of Brunswick County, North Carolina* (1978). Lee spent his teaching career, from 1956 to 1977, at The Citadel in Charleston, South Carolina, where he served a term as chairman of the history department. In addition, he was president of the South Carolina Historical Society. Upon retirement he remained in Charleston until 1992, when he returned to his beloved Lower Cape Fear. Lawrence Lee died in Wilmington on October 18, 1996.

While a graduate student, Lee presented a paper titled "Old Brunswick, the Story of a Colonial Town" to the 1951 meeting of the North Carolina Literary and Historical Association. He called for an archaeological investigation of the abandoned site, which had been relatively untouched for nearly two centuries, and concluded by observing that

"Brunswick could well be the counterpart of the Jamestown
excavations." He began to work at the site on his own in
1952 and for a number of years thereafter. Archaeologist
Stanley South later evaluated Lee's role: "Working with the
United States Army Corps of Engineers, the State of North
Carolina, J. Laurence Sprunt, and the Diocese of East Carolina (Episcopal), he was largely instrumental in the estab-
lishment in 1955 of Brunswick Town State Historic Site. . . ."
At present Brunswick Town is among the most visited of the
sites operated by the Historic Sites Section of the Division of
Archives and History. The people of North Carolina and in
particular the Division of Archives and History owe a great
debt to Lawrence Lee. The reprinting of *Indian Wars in North
Carolina, 1663-1763* is a small payment on that debt.

Jerry C. Cashion
Research Supervisor
Division of Archives and History

February 1997

CHAPTER I

The Land of the Indians

Many years ago North Carolina was a battlefield on which its native people fought to survive. The greater portion of this struggle took place in the century between 1663 and 1763. At the beginning of this period North Carolina became an English colony when King Charles II granted it to eight of his loyal followers, the Lords Proprietors. It was then an almost unbroken forest that stretched westward from the sea coast over the low and flat Coastal Plain; across the rolling hills of the Piedmont Plateau and up and over the lofty mountains of the west. At the time of the grant to the Lords Proprietors, a few white settlers had already begun to come into the area. To them, and to others who followed for many years thereafter, this forest was both a friend and a foe. On one hand, it provided timber and fuel, food and medicine, and many other things necessary to life. When cleared, it also provided land for cultivation. But endless toil was the price of a share of this treasure of nature. Courage, too, was needed, because the forest also sheltered the native Indians, to whom it had long been a home and who were not willing to have it taken from them.

Within the forest the Indians lived a primitive life in which they depended on nature to supply their simple needs. Suddenly, they were confronted with a more complicated way of life known as Western Civilization which the whites brought with them from Europe and which they sought to transplant on American soil. The ways of life of the two races were too different for one race to accept that of the other. As a result, a struggle over possession of the land followed. In this struggle, it was the good fortune of the whites that their advanced civilization was the more power-ful. It was the misfortune of the Indians that the more ad-vanced civilization was also the more destructive. Before the relentless white tide, the Indians were eventually crushed, but not before they had shed their own blood and the blood of countless whites. To the very end, the Indian fought to save his home and his people.

In his struggle for survival, the Indian has emerged as a savage villain. In part, this is because certain of his prac-tices were cruel and barbarous when measured by the stand-ards of Western Civilization. In part, it is because the story of the conflict between the two races has been told by white men who alone possessed a written language to record it. The story has become distorted because those who recorded it were generally too close to the horrors of the conflict to view the enemy with sympathy and understanding. Never-theless, it is a story that can be seen in its true proportions only with some knowledge of the Indians as human beings. Fortunately, from the pens of certain writers of the time we are able to learn something of these people and of their way of life. Among the earliest of these writers was John Lawson, naturalist and historian, who lived and travelled among them.

CHAPTER II

The Indians of North Carolina

When Europeans first arrived in North Carolina there were only three important tribes, or nations, in the region. In the order of their size they were the Cherokee of the western mountains, the largest; the Catawba Nation of the Piedmont Plateau and the Tuscarora of the Coastal Plain. The Cherokee and Tuscarora were members of the Iroquoian language group while the Catawba were Siouan. As settlers moved westward from the coast they came into contact with these tribes at different times and, because of their location, the Coastal Plain Indians were the first to attract attention. In addition to the Tuscarora, the natives of this region included several small tribes that were important only because they existed at a time when the white settlers were also few.

About 1660, the Coastal Plain Indians numbered approximately 30,000. About a half century later, rum, small-pox and intertribal warfare had reduced them to no more than 5,000, which was about the same as the white population of the time. From John Lawson and other sources we learn something of the distribution of the Indian population about 1710. The largest tribe, the Tuscarora, numbered about 4,000 persons, including between 1,200 and 1,400 warriors. At some unknown time in the past, they had separated from their kinsmen, the Iroquoian Five Nations Confederation in the north, and at Lawson's time they occupied an extensive inland area stretching from the upper Neuse northward to the Roanoke River. They also hunted as far south as Cape Fear. A few miles to the south of the Tuscarora the Woccon, a Siouan tribe of about 350 persons, lived, and to the northward there were about 150 Meherrin Indians, an Iroquoian tribe living along the Meherrin River. Eastward, and extending southward from the Virginia border to the Neuse River there were several Algonquian tribes, members of a separate language group with a total population of perhaps 500 persons. The Chowanoc, Pasquotank, Poteskeet and Yeopim, about 200 in all, lived above the Albemarle Sound. The remaining 300, members of the Pamlico, Hatteras, Matchapunga and Bay, or Bear, River tribes were located below the Sound. The Neusioc and Coree, Iroquoian tribes located on the Neuse River and Core Sound, had a combined population of about 125 people. Farther to the southward the Cape Fears, a Siouan tribe of about 200 members, lived along the lower Cape Fear, but were considered South Carolina Indians.

In addition to the Indians who lived on the Coastal Plain there were also outside tribes which came in from time to time to make war on the local natives. Of these invaders, the most feared were warriors of the Five Nations Confederation of New York, usually identified as the Seneca, the name of a member tribe. The Shawnee of the north and west were also frequent and destructive visitors.

In the beginning, the Indians usually welcomed the Europeans as friends with whom they could share the land. Too late to save themselves, they realized the whites did not wish to share but to possess alone. The Lords Proprietors repeatedly urged the colonists to cultivate friendly relations with the natives, but the colonists refused to follow the advice. Strange to say, they came to look upon the natives as intruders even though, as John Lawson wrote, "We have abandoned our own Native Soil, to drive them out, and possess theirs." The whites also looked upon the Indians "with Scorn and Disdain, and think them little better than Beasts in Human Shape." Far from being "Beasts in Human

THE INDIANS OF NORTH CAROLINA

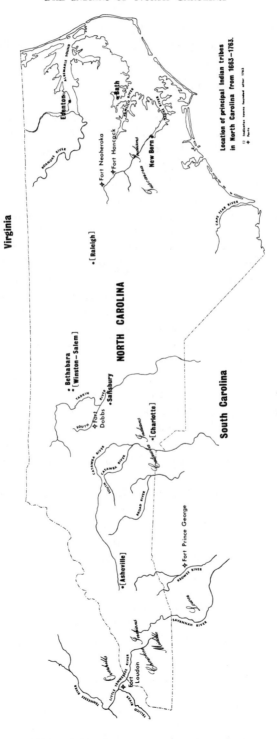

Location of principal Indian tribes in North Carolina from 1663–1763.

[ ] Indicates towns founded after 1763
✦ Forts

Shape," the natives were fine specimens of humanity who were described by their friend, Lawson, in the following words:

The Indians of North-Carolina are a well shaped clean-made People, of different Statures, as the Europeans are, yet chiefly inclined to be tall. They are a very straight People, and never bend forwards or stoop in the Shoulders, unless much overpowered by old Age. Their limbs are exceeding well shaped. Their Bodies are a little flat, which is occasioned by being laced down to a Board in their Infancy . . . Their Eyes are black, or of a dark Hazel; The White is marbled with red Streaks, which is ever common to these People . . . Their [skin] Colour is of a tawny, which would not be so dark did they not dawb themselves with Bear's Oil, and a Colour like burnt Cork. This is begun in their Infancy and continued for a long time, which fills the Pores and enables them better to endure the Extremity of the Weather. They are never bald on their Heads, although never so old, which I believe, proceeds from their Heads being always uncovered, and the greasing their Hair, so often as they do, with Bear's Fat, which is a great Nourisher of the Hair, and causes it to grow very fast. Amongst the Bear's Oil (when they intend to be fine) they mix a certain red Powder, that comes from a Scarlet Root . . . With this and Bear's Grease they anoint their Heads and Temples, which is esteemed as ornamental . . . Their Eyes are commonly full and manly, and their Gate sedate and majestic . . . They are dexterous and steady, both as to their Hands and Feet, to Admiration. They will walk over deep Brooks and Creeks on the smallest Poles, and without any Fear or Concern . . . In Running, Leaping or any such other Exercise, their Legs seldom miscarry and give them a Fall; and as for letting anything fall out of their Hands, I never yet knew one Example. I never saw a Dwarf amongst them, nor but one that was Hump-backed. Their teeth are yellow with Smoking Tobacco, which both

Men and Women are much addicted to . . . They have
no Hairs on their Faces, (except some few) and those
but little . . . They are continually plucking it away
from their Faces by the Roots . . . As there are found
very few, or scarce any, Deformed or Cripples amongst
them, so neither did I ever see but one blind Man;
and then they would give me no Account how his Blind-
ness came . . . No People have better Eyes, or see better
in the Night or Day than the Indians. Some alledge
that the Smoke of the Pitch-Pine which they chiefly
burn, does both preserve and strengthen the Eyes . . .
They let their Nails grow very long, which they reckon,
is the Use Nails are designed for, and laugh at the
Europeans for paring theirs, which, they say disarms
them of that which Nature designed them for. They
are not of so robust and strong Bodies as to lift great
Burdens, and endure Labour and Slavish Work, as the
Europeans are; yet some that are Slaves, prove very
good and laborious; But of themselves, they never work
as the English do, taking care for no farther than what
is absolutely necessary to support Life. In Traveling
and Hunting, they are very indefatigable, because that
carries a Pleasure along with the Profit. I have known
some of them very strong; and as for Running and Leaping, they are extraordinary Fellows, and will dance for
several Nights together with the greatest Briskness imag-
inable, their Wind never failing them.

Other writers generally agreed with Lawson as to the
physical characteristics of the Indians though some described
their skin as reddish-brown or copper. The description of
the Cherokee complexion as olive might have been due to
an illusion created by their practice of pricking gunpowder
into their skins to produce decorative patterns. The Cherokee, like certain other tribes, also had a distinctive hair style
to identify their tribal connection. The Cherokee men
plucked or shaved all the hair from their heads except for
a tuft on the back which was decorated with beads and

feathers and such. These variations, however, were differences in detail only, and one early writer who was familiar
with the various tribes said of them, "there is but little
diversity with respect to complexion, manners, or customs."

The Indians of North Carolina were agricultural people
who also depended on hunting and fishing. To follow these
pursuits, each tribe occupied as much land as it needed or
could hold. The tribal land, or "nation," was the common
property of all the members with specific areas allocated to
the various towns in which the people lived. They were
located on the banks of streams which were useful for travel,
fishing and other purposes. These towns varied in size from
a few to 200 or more houses and each had a state, or town
house for religious and other ceremonial uses. The larger
towns sometimes extended over an area of several miles with
the buildings scattered among fields and orchards. The cultivation of the fields was the responsibility of the tribe, and
the work and the harvest was shared. Corn was the principal
crop but various types of vegetables were also grown. In
addition to the common fields, each family had its own small
plot, or garden, upon which its dwelling stood. Among the
eastern Indians the dwellings were frames of poles covered
with bark. Those of the Cherokee in the more rigorous
climate of the western mountains were covered with clay.

While the cultivation of the fields was the main occupation
during the warm months, hunting was the principal activity
during the winter months. Hunting was sometimes done
individually or in small parties, but it was often carried on
in the nature of a large expedition. The most expert young
men were chosen for the actual hunting while the less capable
young men and the young women went along to serve the
hunters. The old people were left behind to care for the
town. In the autumn of the year, as soon as the leaves had

fallen and the woods were dry, the hunting parties went out and sometimes stayed for many days. At a chosen place the woods were set afire and the deer and other game were driven into a restricted area and killed with ease. The use of fire in this manner was destructive to the woods and endangered property when carried on near the settlements. Consequently, it was a source of friction between the Indians and the whites. Nevertheless, hunting provided additional food for the people and the surplus meat, along with grain, vegetables and fruits were dried and placed in the town storehouses for future use. Clearly, these Indian towns were not temporary camps of a people wandering about in a wilderness world. They were small farm communities in which the people in times of peace lived a reasonably stable existence.

The degree of orderliness that the Indians achieved in their life was due largely to their government. Each town had its own headman, or chief, who the English usually called "king." In some cases this title was hereditary but usually, and particularly in later years, the position was elective. The king was assisted by lesser war captains and councillors, who were also elected on the basis of ability, and all important decisions were made by the leaders meeting in council. Each town was independent of the other and while they ordinarily acted in unison, they did not always do so. The degree of conformity differed among various groups. The government of the Iroquoian tribes seems to have been less forceful than that among the Siouan and Algonquian tribes.

The life of the Indians before the coming of the whites was a simple one in which they supplied their own needs through nature, and with their own hands and crude instruments. After the coming of the whites, their existence became complicated by the use of European products. Machine-made textiles came to be used for clothing in place of skins and furs which were traded to the whites for their goods. Ancient crafts were abandoned and often forgotten in favor of the use of manufactured tools. The bow and arrow was put aside in favor of the more destructive gun. In becoming dependent upon things they could not produce themselves, the Indians became dependent on the whites who could and did produce them. This dependence increased the longer the association continued. By the time the natives realized they had lost their self-reliance, it was too late to turn back. At any point they might have resumed the old ways of peacetime, but their life was not always one of peace. And in war, they had no choice. Faced with enemies, both white and red, who used guns, self-preservation required the use of the same destructive weapons. Guns, in turn, required a constant supply of ammunition and this became the most vital need of the Indians and their greatest weakness. Without it they were helpless, even in peace. Furs and skins were the price of ammunition, and ammunition was used to provide the furs and skins. Forced to trade with the whites for guns and ammunition, the natives continued to accept their dependence for other needs. As a consequence, the Indians were in bondage to the whites long before they were defeated on the field of battle.

In their struggle to survive in the wilderness world in which they lived, the Indians were faced with many enemies and warfare had become a tradition with them. The coming of the whites only increased its intensity. Until they developed a desire for European goods, the Indians seldom fought for material gain. Instead, war was usually a means of gaining glory or vengeance. The natives were a very revengeful people and seldom forgot a wrong until they had obtained satisfaction. This desire was perhaps the weakest aspect of their character. Regardless of the causes, though, war to them was a serious matter and was entered into only after solemn deliberation. Once a decision for war was made, a stick painted red was sent around to the other towns of the tribe, and even to other friendly tribes as an invitation to join in the coming struggle. Some tribes used pipes for this purpose. Other used tomahawks, or hatchets, and would "bury the hatchet" with the coming of peace.

Military duty was not required, but desire for glory and the fear of disapproval were enough to encourage most men to serve. Even women went to war and sometimes achieved distinction. In preparing for battle the Indians discarded all unnecessary clothing and equipment and ordinarily carried with them only their weapons and food in the form of parched corn and dried meat. Some went on the warpath afoot. Others, like the Cherokee, used horses. Either way they were fearsome sights as a result of painting their faces and other parts of their bodies with red and black colors which made them resemble "devils coming out of Hell." These colors had symbolic meanings; red for the blood of war and black for death which the enemy might expect. The colors not only served to create terror but also to disguise the individual warrior. On the other hand, some mark or other evidence was usually left behind after every attack to identify the tribe that had struck the blow.

Indians usually fought only in small groups. Even when large numbers went out to war, they generally divided into small parties and their scalping knives and tomahawks, which were also manufactured in Europe, were almost as important as their guns. They also rarely fought in open battle and looked upon the English practice of doing so as foolish. Instead, they struck from behind cover and faded back into the forest, if necessary, so they might strike again. This practice was not due to lack of courage. It was simply the most sensible method of forest fighting. Too, the Indian custom of attacking at dawn was not because of superstitious fear of spirits that might wander in the dark. Dawn was ordinarily the best time to surprise the enemy. These and other fighting tactics had been developed over a period of many years. They were used against native enemies and they were also used against the whites.

In warfare nothing influenced the Indians more than religion. All groups did not agree in every detail, but there was much similarity in their beliefs. Some believed in one supreme God, the maker of all things, who rewarded the good and punished the bad. Others believed that all good came from the Good Spirit and all bad from the Evil Spirit. The Cherokee, it was said, "adored the sun and the moon, but really worshipped the God who made all."

It was also a Cherokee chief who said that the Indians had "as good an idea of a *future state* as any white man." This was a belief that was shared by the Indians of the coastal area. The Hell of these people was a land of cold and hunger and ugly women. Their Heaven was a land of abundance and contentment; of eternal youth and good hunting where "every Month is May" and "the women are bright as Stars, and never scold." With the prospect of such a future life, the Indians usually faced death with resignation. This was especially true when it was inflicted by the enemy. In fact, this idea of the life hereafter explains, at least in part, the treatment of their victims in time of war.

In battle the enemy was usually killed but captives were sometimes taken. Some were kept as slaves and some were sold as such. Some were held for vengeance. Punishment could not be inflicted by the European practice of imprisonment. Even if the Indians had been inclined to follow the practice, their buildings were not suitable for it. Consequently, the fate of the victims was death. But to the Indians a quick death was less punishment than it was a painless passage to the happy life after death. Vengeance demanded pain before death. To gain this revenge, the Indians usually tortured their captives and sometimes in indescribable fashion. The methods were left to the women of the tribe to satisfy their grief for the loss of their men. Regardless of how just the natives might have thought it, this practice, more than any other, caused the whites to look upon the Indians as a brutal and savage race.

CHAPTER III

Early Indian Wars 1663-1711

The first permanent English inhabitants of North Carolina came down from Virginia about 1660 and occupied the area to the north of Albemarle Sound, which was then called Albemarle County. For some years they were few in number, and fortunately for them so were the Indians. Only the Chowanoc were strong enough at the time to have turned them back, but by a treaty made in 1663, that tribe agreed to peace. The settlers who came to the Cape Fear region shortly thereafter were not so fortunate.

The earliest recorded visit of the English to Cape Fear occurred in the fall of 1662 when William Hilton, representing a group of New Englanders interested in settling in the south, explored the river and its northeast branch. During the course of his visit Hilton came into contact with less than 100 Indians and these he considered to be weak and timid people. Hilton was impressed with the Cape Fear country and, according to the custom of the time, he purchased the land from the natives in the name of those he represented. Soon thereafter a number of New Englanders came down to Cape Fear to settle but returned north after only a short stay. Why they left is not known definitely, but some seventy years later a writer explained that they had been driven away by the local Indians. A hasty departure is indicated by the fact that they left behind their cattle and swine. They also left a note on a post advising others not to settle there.

In the summer of 1663, Hilton returned to the Cape Fear River to explore it again for a group on the far-away island of Barbados. This time he also went up the northwest branch, as well as the northeast, and found the Indians to be more numerous and more spirited than on his previous visit. He again purchased the land from the natives, this time in the name of the Barbadians, and sailed away to make another glowing report of the region.

In May, 1664, settlers again arrived in the Cape Fear country which had been named Clarendon County. Within a year or two the scattered homestead of colonists from Barbados, and of others from New England and elsewhere, stretched along the river for a distance of sixty miles. For awhile it appeared that this attempt at settlement would succeed, but it did not. For various reasons the colony was neglected by the Lords Proprietors and by those on the island of Barbados who had been expected to support it. Before the end of 1666, the inhabitants of Clarendon County found themselves in serious difficulties for want of supplies. And they added to their troubles by abusing the Indians. It was said, a half-century later, the settlers had seized and sent away Indian children "under Pretense of instructing them in Learning and the Principles of the Christian Religion." More likely, they were sent away as slaves. But whatever the reason, the natives resented the taking of their children and showed their resentment by turning in violence on the whites.

In the Clarendon County War that followed, the colonists had the advantage of firearms to use against the primitive bows and arrows of the natives. The Indians, however, found a strong ally in their determination to rid themselves of the white intruders. They relentlessly continued to attack the colonists and their property until the colonists finally gave up in desperation and abandoned the settlement in 1667. The region once again became Indian country and remained so for many years.

Along with their homes and fields, the Clarendon colonists

left behind natives with bitter memories. For many years, they showed this bitterness by abusing whites unfortunate enough to be shipwrecked on the shores of Cape Fear. By the 1690's, though, the Cape Fear Indians had become so troubled by attacks from other tribes that they appealed to the government of Carolina for protection. This protection was granted on the condition that the Indians treat ship-wrecked refugees with better care in the future. This agreement marked the renewal of friendly relations between the Cape Fear Indians and the whites which lasted for many years.

Except for a possible minor outbreak in 1666, the people of Albemarle County were spared the horror of Indian warfare until about 1675. At that time certain of the Indians of Virginia were in conflict with the settlers there and persuaded the Chowanoc that they should drive the whites from Albemarle County. Ignoring the treaty of friendship of 1663, the Chowanoc turned on the settlers and in the war that followed, both sides suffered heavy losses. The Indians were faced with the awesome guns of the whites while the settlers, in their isolated homesteads, lived in constant fear of attack. Too, Indians "haunting" the forests made travel a dangerous venture. The Chowanoc War had dragged on for about two years when the tide of victory turned in favor of the colonists with the arrival of a ship laden with arms and ammunition. The complete defeat of the Chowanoc followed in the summer of 1677. They were then moved from their ancestral home on the Meherrin River to a reservation on Bennett's Creek.

For many years the colonists did not venture far from the coast, but they did gradually expand their area of occupation southward. Because roads were few, or non-existent, the settlers sometimes by-passed extensive areas to establish their

homes on the banks of the next navigable stream that would
provide them with a convenient means of transportation.

Because of this system of settlement, many miles of lonely
wilderness often separated one group of colonists from the
nearest European neighbors. As a result, the various areas of
settlement, particularly those on the outer edge of white occupation, were more exposed to Indian attack than they would
have been had the settlers remained close together. The loss
of this strength of unity was especially dangerous in view
of the fact the Indians usually occupied the land along the
streams desired by the whites, and for the same reason. This
competition over small areas of the most desirable land
brought the two races into open conflict sooner than might
have been the case had one or both been satisfied with any
kind of land.

The creation of separate and isolated areas of settlement
can be traced in the actual movement of the Europeans
southward. By 1675, colonists had already crossed over and
occupied the south shore of Albemarle Sound. By 1691, others
had settled along the Pamlico River, leaving between them
and Albemarle Sound "about fifty miles desert to pass
through, without any human creature inhabiting it." This
"desert" remained unoccupied for many years. By 1703, or
soon thereafter, other colonists had crossed over the Pamlico
River and were settled on the Neuse. This was the southern
limit of settlement at the time and the area above Cape
Fear had become known as North Carolina to distinguish it
from the Lords Proprietors' land below Cape Fear known
as South Carolina.

South Carolina was begun in 1670 when a few colonists
founded Charles Town, later Charleston, on the Ashley
River, in the midst of a number of small Indian tribes. Those
to the north were Siouan and those to the south were Musk-

hogean, a separate language group. As it grew, South Carolina became the southern frontier of the English continental colonies. As such, it protected North Carolina against the Spaniards of Florida, and the French of Louisiana, and also against the powerful Creek, Choctaw and Chickasaw Indians who occupied a vast inland area reaching to the Mississippi River. For many years the people of South Carolina remained close to the coast, but from the great port of Charles Town its Indian traders carried on their business far into the interior. By means of this trade, many tribes came under the control or influence of the South Carolina government long before white settlement reached them. Among these tribes were the Catawba and the Cherokee who lived partly in North Carolina. North Carolina, long without an adequate seaport, never developed an Indian trade beyond the Coastal Plain and never made any real effort to extend its authority over the Catawba and Cherokee.

Land was an important cause of trouble between the Indians and the whites, but it was not the only cause. Ill-feeling also resulted from trading activities between the two races because, according to John Lawson, the white traders "daily cheat them in everything we sell, and esteem it a Gift of Christianity not to sell them so cheap as we do to the Christians, as we call ourselves." The whites also enslaved the natives, and this practice was possibly the greatest of all the causes of Indian resentment. Many of these Indian slaves were sold outside the colony and were probably sent to the port of Charles Town, in South Carolina, for shipment to more distant places. To hear the name "Ashley River" was enough to fill a North Carolina Indian with fear that he would be taken there.

The Indians, on the other hand, were not always without blame. Unfortunately, they acquired the vices of the white people more readily than the virtues. In fact, each race brought out the worst in the other. The Indians rarely stole from each other, but they saw no evil in taking the property of the colonists. By burning the woods on hunting expeditions near settled areas, the natives destroyed desirable timber and, sometimes, the homes of the whites. Indians along the coast often abused fishermen and shipwreck survivors. The wrongs of the natives were not so great as the wrongs they suffered, but they did add to the growing antagonism between the two races. The natives were expected to follow the English ideas of right and wrong, but nothing was done to teach those ideas to them. The settlers of early North Carolina made no real effort to Christianize the Indians. If they had, they might have created understanding that could have spared both races much tragedy and grief.

By 1703, bad relations between the white and red races had become serious, especially in the Pamlico River area. The Bay River and Matchapunga Indians were becoming more and more aggressive and insolent in taking the property of the colonists. The Coree Indians had become so abusive in their conduct that the North Carolina government declared war on them. This was not an important war, but there seemed to be a danger that a far more serious one would follow. The Indians suspected the refusal of the whites to sell them guns and ammunition was because the whites intended to make general war on them. In the winter of 1704 there were widespread reports that the powerful Tuscarora were plotting with other nearby tribes to destroy the colonists. The people of the Pamlico River area became so frightened they appealed to the government for immediate protection. As a result, Robert Daniel, the deputy-governor, called the various Indian leaders in for a meeting. At the meeting it was agreed that both races would keep the peace.

This agreement probably prevented a serious war at the time, but it did not settle the real differences between the Indians and the colonists. In the next few years relations became even worse, and the Tuscarora decided they would rather leave North Carolina than to continue to live under the conditions that existed. In 1710, they sent messengers to the officials of Pennsylvania asking permission to settle in that colony. They gave as the principal reason for the request their desire to be able to move about freely and to hunt in the forest without the constant fear of murder or enslavement. The Pennsylvania officials agreed to permit the move provided the Indians obtain a certificate of their good behavior in the past from the North Carolina government. Their failure to obtain the certificate resulted in one of the great tragedies of North Carolina history. Unable to escape from oppression, the Tuscarora turned in violence on their oppressors.

CHAPTER IV

The Tuscarora War; The Barnwell Expedition 1711-1712

The Tuscarora War was the most terrible Indian war that ever took place in North Carolina. The Indians struck in the autumn of 1711, and they could hardly have chosen a more advantageous time. The colonists were divided by political disagreement. Edward Hyde had come over from England the previous year to administer the colony as deputy governor. His right to the post was disputed by Thomas Cary who had previously held the office. In the dispute that followed, known as Cary's Rebellion, Hyde and Cary both attracted supporters who actually took up arms against each other. The colony was in the midst of civil war.

The Rebellion ended in the summer of 1711, but there was already evidence of serious unrest among the Indians. At the beginning of the year, the Meherrin had been reported as becoming more and more insolent. By mid-summer this attitude had spread to other tribes. At the same time, it was said that Cary supporters had offered rich rewards to the Tuscarora to attack the followers of Hyde. It was also said that the young men of the tribe had agreed to the offer but had been overruled by the old men. This latter report seems to have lulled the settlers into a false sense of security.

According to one prominent colonist, the increasing hostile attitude of the natives was because the whites "cheated these Indians in trading, and would not allow them to hunt near their plantations, and under that pretense took away from them their game, arms and ammunition." A more immediate cause might have been the founding of the town of New

Bern in 1710 by Baron Christoph von Graffenried, the leader of a group of Swiss and Germans settling the area.

New Bern was established on the site of a Neusioc Indian town called Chattooka, or Cartouca. The natives who occupied the land were paid for it and they moved away, but apparently they were not satisfied. As Surveyor-General of the colony, John Lawson surveyed the site. According to von Graffenried, the site had also been chosen for him by Lawson who claimed it to be uninhabited. When it was found to be occupied by Indians, he charged the Surveyor-General with recommending they be driven off without payment. These accusations were not in keeping with Lawson's otherwise sympathetic attitude towards the natives, but, if true, they might explain the terrible fate he met soon thereafter.

In mid-September, 1711, Lawson invited von Graffenried to go with him on a trip up the Neuse. The purpose of the trip was to examine the river and to seek a better route to Virginia. Lawson assured the Baron there would be no danger from the Indians, but the prospect of such a route through, or near, their hunting grounds could have been a matter of great concern to the Indians. In any event, several days after their departure, both men were seized by the natives and taken to Catechna, the Tuscarora town of King Hancock, on Contentea Creek. After questioning the prisoners, the Indians decided to set them free. Before they were to leave the following day, the captives were questioned again. The King of Cartouca, the New Bern site, reproached Lawson who answered in anger. A general quarrel followed in which von Graffenried did not take part, but both he and Lawson were again confined. At another council meeting, the Indians decided to execute Lawson and to free the Baron who had promised presents for his freedom. Von Graffenried did not see it and the natives were very secretive about the manner of Lawson's death. Some said he was hanged and others said his throat was slit with a razor he carried with him. It was generally believed the Indians "stuck him full of fine small splinters of touchwood, like hogs' bristles, and so set him gradually on fire."

The day after Lawson's execution, the Indians told von Graffenried that he would not be released for some time, because they had decided to make war on the people of North Carolina and especially those on the Pamlico, Neuse and Trent Rivers, and on Core Sound. He would have to remain with them until their work had been completed. King Hancock was the leader of the conspiracy and he had persuaded the lower Tuscarora towns to join him. The northern, or upper Tuscarora towns, about equal in number to the lower towns, refused to take part in the conflict. King Tom Blount, the chief of one of the upper towns, was friendly with the colonists and exercised some influence over the chiefs of the other nearby towns. King Hancock, however, was supported by the several small tribes in the Neuse-Pamlico area. These included the Coree, Matchapunga, Pamlico, Bear River and Neusioc Indians. The Coree and Neusioc had recently moved inland from their old towns to be nearer the Tuscarora, and the other tribes had probably done the same. Five hundred warriors of these various tribes gathered at Catechna, or Hancock's Town, for the attack.

At sunrise on the morning of September 22, 1711, the blow fell. Divided into small war parties, the Indians swept down the Neuse and along the south shore of the Pamlico. Two hours later, 130 colonists lay dead, about the same number on each stream. Some were tortured horribly; others were desecrated after death. Many were left wounded. The less fortunate were taken captive. The rest of the people fled for their lives, leaving the bodies of their loved ones to be eaten by wolves and vultures. In their violence, the Indians had no regard for age or sex. After several days of slaughter and destruction, the enemy drew back into Hancock's Town to rest for further violence. With them, they took plunder and captives, including women and children.

On that tragic September morning, the people of North Carolina found themselves in the midst of a war they were not prepared to fight. In spite of past danger signals, they had made no preparations for possible hostilities. Nowhere in the whole colony was there a fortified place to which the people might flee to safety. There were few men with military training. Neither war supplies nor food had been stored for emergency use. The Indians seemed better supplied with ammunition than the colonists, and a bad drought combined with neglect of the fields during Cary's Rebellion had resulted in a serious shortage of food. The trade of the colony had almost ceased and there was little money or credit with which to import clothing and other necessities which were scarce and badly needed. Worst of all, political differences still divided the people, making it impossible for the government to act with necessary speed and responsibility.

With the first attack of the enemy, the colonists gathered together in certain plantation homes to gain strength from unity. A number of these dwellings were fortified as were the towns of Bath and New Bern. Within a month there were eleven such fortified garrisons in the colony. They were manned by untrained civilians. With the majority of the whites confined in their shelters, Indian warriors ravaged the countryside. Homes were plundered and burned. Livestock was slaughtered. Fences and the fields they enclosed were destroyed. And wherever they could be found, whites were killed. Destruction was widespread and sometimes came within sight of the garrisons. On occasions, even the garrisons were attacked.

To the terrified colonists, the cause seemed hopeless. The men, however courageous, were untrained and inexperienced in Indian fighting. Trapped as they were in scattered garrisons, a body large enough to strike back at the enemy with effectiveness could not be raised. And it was not wise for the few men in the individual garrisons to venture out among several hundred hostile Indians. The men of one detachment did go out and attempted to fight the enemy in open battle. The result was one dead and the majority wounded before the surviving whites could flee to safety. On another occasion, a detachment went out from Brice's garrison on the Trent River to engage a nearby group of hostiles. While it was out, other Indians attacked the weakened garrison. Fortunately, they were repelled without serious loss. Because they knew the peculiar techniques of native warfare, Indians were better qualified than whites to fight Indians. The great need of the people of North Carolina was native allies to help them in their struggle. But there were none.

Of the various North Carolina tribes, only the upper Tuscarora were numerous enough to be helpful and they were not to be trusted. Though they had taken no active part in the conflict, they were suspected of knowing of the conspiracy and consenting to it. They might eventually serve as useful allies, but, first, they would have to prove themselves trustworthy. In the meantime, it was feared the success of the hostiles might encourage them to join in the war against the whites. Equally disturbing was the news that numerous warriors of the Five Nations were coming south to live with the hostile Tuscarora and aid them in their war. As owners of the colony, the Lords Proprietors were responsible for its defense, but they did nothing. Unable to defend itself, North Carolina turned to its neighbors, Virginia and South Carolina, for help.

Upon hearing of the calamity that had befallen North Carolina, Governor Alexander Spotswood of Virginia stopped all trade from that colony with the Indians and sent members of the militia to the Virginia frontier to prevent the Virginia Indians from joining the enemy. He then persuaded the Virginia legislature to appropriate funds for aid to North Carolina. Spotswood also used the prestige of his colony and the Indian hope for the resumption of its trade in an effort to persuade the upper Tuscarora to fight the enemy, or to remain neutral.

The plea that went to the government of South Carolina was for Indian allies. In making this request, North Carolina's Governor Hyde was following an established policy of all European nations in America: the use of Indians against Indians. There were several advantages to this policy. Not only were Indians more effective than whites in fighting Indians, but, in doing so, they relieved the whites of the hazardous task. At times, too, the practice served to divert native hostility that otherwise might have been directed against the whites. To gain the cooperation of the Indians, the colonists played on the strong spirit of rivalry among the natives. Divided into numerous groups, the great weakness of the Indians was their inability to unite and remain united.

The whites also played on the increasing desire of the natives for English trade goods. They purchased captured Indian enemies as slaves and also paid for scalps in order to encourage their allies to kill as well as capture. In this way, scalps became a form of money as well as marks of glory. The prospect of Tuscarora slaves and scalps was the lure that the Governor of North Carolina held out to the Indians of South Carolina.

Within a month of the first attack, an agent from North Carolina, Major Christopher Gale, was in Charles Town with the appeal for aid. The South Carolina legislature responded by appropriating a substantial sum of money. It also agreed to raise an army of friendly Indians, with white officers, to send to North Carolina. Major Gale promised to meet the expedition on the Neuse River with an army of white North Carolinians. He also promised that food would be supplied.

Soon afterwards, the South Carolina army moved northward under the command of Colonel John Barnwell. On the long overland march through the interior, many of Barnwell's Indians deserted, but others joined him. Some had no weapons other than bows and arrows. When he reached the Neuse in late January, 1712, his force consisted of 30 white men and nearly 500 Indians. His own Yamassee Company of more than 150 men contained 87 Yamassee from the Savannah River as well as warriors of several other small Muskhogean tribes to the south of Charles Town. The other companies, containing almost 350 men, were made up of warriors of the various Siouan tribes to the north of Charles Town. Among the tribes represented were the Catawba, Saraw (or Cheraw), Wateree, Wynyaw and Cape Fear.

When Barnwell arrived at the agreed meeting place, the men promised by Gale were not there to meet him. Only a short time before, the colony's legislature, divided by continued political differences, had refused to provide either men or supplies for the expedition. In fact, it had failed to take any steps to defend the colony. Disappointed and without guides familiar with the country, Barnwell pushed on towards the Tuscarora town of Narhantes, hoping to take it by surprise. Described by him as the most warlike town of the Tuscarora, Narhantes was an open village with farms scattered over an area of several miles. About the town were nine small palisaded forts. Some newly built and others under construction, these forts stood about a mile apart. He attacked the strongest of the enclosures and after breaking through the outer walls found two houses therein that were stronger than the walls. Among the most desperate of the defenders were a number of native women who fought with bows and arrows. Within half an hour the fort had fallen. Of the fifty-two enemy killed, at least ten were women. Thirty were taken captive and the remainder abandoned the town and its forts, leaving behind much plunder that had been taken from the colonists. Barnwell's casualties were seven killed and thirty-two wounded. A more serious loss was the desertion of many of his Indians who took the captives and plunder and slipped away. Before leaving Narhantes several days later, Barnwell destroyed it along with its forts and five nearby towns as well.

From Narhantes, Barnwell marched through the Tuscarora country to Bath Town on the Pamlico River where he arrived on February 10th. On the way, he passed through a number of enemy towns and did considerable damage. He also took a number of enemy scalps. Property seized along the line of march proved to be a costly prize. Loaded with plunder, many more of his Indians slipped away.

Late in February, Barnwell was joined by sixty-seven North Carolinians. Their arrival increased his strength to 94 whites and 148 Indians. Most of the Indians were of Barnwell's own Yamassee Company. The new arrivals also created a problem, because they came without food and the scarcity of food was already a matter of grave concern to Barnwell. The following day, Barnwell set out for Hancock's Town, hoping to take it along with any food that might be there. His horses and heavy baggage were left behind near Bath Town. On March 1st, he arrived at Hancock's Town only to find it deserted. On the opposite bank of Contentea Creek, however, the enemy had constructed a strong, palisaded fort. Within the enclosure were 130 warriors and a call had gone out for other hostiles to join them. Their families and white captives were hidden in a nearby swamp.

On March 5th, Barnwell attacked Hancock's Fort, confident of taking it. Instead, he found himself forced to agree to a truce. Prior to the attack, the Indians had brought at least some of their white captives into the fort. During the attack these prisoners were subjected to torture. To the attackers, only a few yards away, the "Cryes and lamentations" of the victims were heart-rending sounds. To Barnwell's shouted demands for the release of the captives, the Indians sent an answer by an English mother with five children in the fort. The attack must be abandoned or the defenders would die fighting and take their prisoners with them. After consultation with his officers, Barnwell accepted this demand on certain conditions. Twelve prisoners were to be delivered to him immediately, and twenty-two more were to be delivered twelve days later at Bachelours Creek, near New Bern. The headmen of the enemy were also to come to Bachelours Creek at the same time to discuss peace.

The day after the truce, Barnwell left Hancock's Fort and four days later arrived in New Bern. On March 19th, the day appointed for the meeting with the enemy, he was sick and sent another in his stead. The enemy did not appear. Angered, Barnwell prepared to strike again. On the Neuse River, near the mouth of Contentea Creek, he built Fort Barnwell on the site of the abandoned Indian village of Core Town. This was the base from which he planned to march once more against Hancock's Fort, only a few miles away. Orders were sent out to the South Carolina Indians who were roaming through the countryside in search of food to come into the fort. Similar orders went to the men of the various garrisons along the Neuse.

On April 1st a message was received from Governor Hyde that men and food were on the way. Hyde added that "a new Turn was given to affairs," and that Barnwell would have no cause to complain in the future. Sometime previously, Barnwell had protested to the North Carolina legislature for its failure to support him. Perhaps stung by this criticism, the legislature took action to defend the colony. A law was passed imposing a fine of five pounds on every man between sixteen and sixty years of age who refused military service. In addition, 4,000 pounds was appropriated for war purposes. A request had also gone to Virginia for 200 men. Hyde's message to Barnwell followed.

Without waiting for the arrival of the relief then being raised by the North Carolina and Virginia governments, Barnwell, in the dark of night of April 7th, moved his troops against Hancock's Fort. His Indians were reduced to 128 warriors, but his whites had increased to 154 by the various garrison detachments. By daylight, his men had surrounded the fort and the second seige had begun. For ten days it continued, and Barnwell was only a few feet from apparent success when, on April 17th, he unaccountably agreed to a conditional surrender of the enemy.

In the more important terms of the peace treaty, the hostiles agreed to give up all captives in the fort immediately and all others within ten days. The same promise was made as to horses, skins and plunder. In the future, they agreed to confine themselves to the area near the fort, and not to hunt or fish in the region between Neuse and the Cape Fear which was to be left to the South Carolina Indians. They also agreed to surrender King Hancock and three other enemy leaders to be named later, but since Hancock had already fled to Virginia, he could not be delivered. In addition, the enemy Indians promised to come in each year in March and pay tribute to the governor of North Carolina. By the payment of this tribute they would acknowledge their continued submission to the government and would become tributary Indians as distinguished from free, or unconquered, Indians.

Barnwell's peace was made without the knowledge or approval of Governor Hyde. His casualties were light and "extreme famine" was the only excuse he gave for not fighting on to complete victory. He said at the time if North Carolina had furnished him with provisions for only four more days he would have "made a glorious end of the war." Governor Hyde, however, felt that hunger hardly justified the failure to pursue a victory that was only a few hours away. Hyde was particularly critical of Barnwell for not waiting for the relief North Carolina had on the way. However justified he might have been, Barnwell was the subject of bitter and widespread criticism in the colony he had done so much to help earlier, and the honors he expected were denied him.

The unpopular peace of Barnwell was not long lasting. Hungry, and disappointed at the few scalps and slaves they had taken, the South Carolina Indians were soon ravaging through the enemy country. According to von Graffenried, Barnwell and his Indians enticed a number of the local natives into Fort Barnwell under pretense of peace. They were then seized and taken to South Carolina to be sold as slaves. This so embittered the rest of the hostiles they "no longer trusted the Christians." Their later behavior seems to bear out the truth of this observation.

CHAPTER V

The Tuscarora War; The Moore Expedition 1712-1715

Soon after Barnwell and his men returned to South Carolina the horror of Indian war once again swept through the Neuse and Pamlico regions. The hostiles, hungry and seeking food, roamed the country taking what they wanted and destroying all else. Many of the inhabitants who ventured back to their plantations were killed. Others went to bed each night with little confidence they would live to see the dawn. The wiser people returned to the security and confinement of fortified garrisons, but even they were not free from attack. Only the generosity of the people of Albemarle County relieved a serious shortage of food in the stricken areas. Under these conditions, inhabitants began to leave the colony. Efforts were made to protect those that remained, but the efforts were not enough.

Barnwell left behind twenty of his Yamassee warriors to patrol the area of recent conflict, and a small armed company was stationed on both the Pamlico and Neuse. A marine company was organized to watch over the waters of Pamlico and Core Sounds. These, however, were only defensive measures that did nothing to end the war. The attempt of the North Carolina officials to encourage military enlistment by imposing a fine was a failure as few men offered their services. The government was not able to raise enough men to rid the colony of the enemy. The troops requested from Virginia never came. With its own frontier also endangered by the same enemy, Virginia was willing to send the men provided North Carolina furnished them with food. North Carolina was too distressed to do so. Later, Virginia sent badly needed clothing for North Carolinians in service, and again offered to send troops provided they were fed. Again, the offer was declined. In the meantime, North Carolina had once more turned to South Carolina for help and received it.

In June, 1712, an agent left North Carolina for Charles Town to request South Carolina to send 1,000 Indians with a few whites and a commander other than Barnwell. In early October, the agent returned with news that the troops were on the way, under the command of Colonel James Moore. Anticipating his aid, North Carolina had already gathered a company of some 140 men on the Neuse River to join the South Carolina troops when they should arrive. This action proved unwise. Moore did not arrive for many weeks and the North Carolinians, too few to attack alone, waited in idleness. Finally, in November, they disbanded and returned to their homes. Their only contribution had been to eat the food that had been sent to the Neuse for the coming expedition. As a result, when the South Carolina army arrived in December, North Carolina was again unprepared. In addition to 33 white men, Moore's army consisted of some 850 Indians. Among these were over 300 Cherokee and 50 Yamassee. The balance included warriors of the various Siouan tribes of the Carolinas. Among the officers was Colonel Moore's brother, Captain Maurice Moore, with the Yamassee Company. To feed such a large body of men was no small problem. Because food was more plentiful in Albemarle County, the men marched there until adequate supplies could be shipped around to the Neuse.

There was also another reason for diverting Moore's forces to Albemarle County. Fear persisted that the Five Nations and the upper Tuscarora would join the enemy. Enemy captives had told Barnwell that the beginning of the war had resulted from the prodding of visiting warriors of the

Five Nations. They had taunted the Tuscarora over their failure to avenge the mistreatment of a drunken Indian by the whites. In the summer of 1712, information was received from the governor of New York that the French in Canada had persuaded the Five Nations to send warriors south to aid the hostile Tuscarora in their war against the English. This concern subsided the following autumn with receipt of information that the New York government had persuaded the Five Nations not to go south. They went to war against the French Indians instead.

The status of the upper Tuscarora, however, remained uncertain. They had not joined the hostiles but neither had they come to the aid of the whites. The government had attempted to persuade them to end the conflict by going to war against the enemy Indians, but they had not done so. King Blount came into the settlements from time to time to declare his continued friendship for the whites, and he alone of the chiefs of the upper towns was trusted. But he could speak for his town only. The government, nevertheless, sought to use his influence with the chiefs of the other towns to persuade them to cooperate with the whites. It was hoped that their desire for the resumption of trade would be sufficient to win them over. The government, however, hesitated to force the issue for fear of driving them to join the hostiles while the colony was in such a weakened condition. The coming of Moore and his army to North Carolina gave its officials the confidence they needed. On a visit to Thomas Pollock, acting governor of North Carolina after the death of Hyde in early September, 1712, Chief Blount expressed his desire for the resumption of trade with his people. He was told that this would be done if they would bring in King Hancock and the scalps of the other hostiles. The offer was accepted after consultation with the headmen of the other neutral towns and King Hancock was delivered and executed. Blount and his people were given until January 1st to bring in the enemy scalps. This allotment of time for the fulfillment of Blount's agreement was permitted by the diversion of Moore's troops to Albemarle County. If Blount succeeded, peace would have been won for the whites. If he failed, Moore could then move out to accomplish the same goal.

If the stay of Moore's forces in Albemarle County solved one problem, it created another. At first his Indians were confined to a designated area where they consumed what food they could find. Then the hungry horde began to spread out over the surrounding country, killing cattle and taking corn. The people of Albemarle County became so disturbed that many of them seemed "more ready to Fall upon the South Carolina Indians, than march against the enemy." They were not only angry but worried also. The danger of using Indians for purposes of war was clearly apparent. The little control that could be exercised over the Indians came from the authority of a single individual, their leader. Some of the more thoughtful people began to consider the possible consequences of the death of this single individual, Colonel Moore. Without a leader, and made up of various tribes and language groups, his Indians would be unrestrained. Such a disorderly band could be as destructive as the enemy it came to fight. January 1st came and Blount had not brought in the scalps of the enemy. Moore then made ready to march against the hostiles. By the middle of the month food had been shipped around to Fort Barnwell, the supply base on the Neuse. On January 17th, Moore's army, enlarged by the addition of some eighty-five North Carolinians, left Albemarle County to the great relief of its inhabitants.

After crossing over Albemarle Sound, Moore headed into the country of the lower Tuscarora where the hostile Indians had already fled to the protection of their forts. Reports indicated the largest concentration of warriors was gathered in Fort Neoheroka, located on a branch of Contentea Creek, a few miles above Hancock's Fort. Accordingly, Neoheroka was the destination of Moore's expedition as it pushed forward through the harsh cold of winter. Progress was slow because of supply difficulties combined with bad weather and deep snow.

Fort Neoheroka was an irregularly shaped enclosure of one and one-half acres contained within a palisaded wall. Along this wall, at strategically located points, were bastions and blockhouses. Within the enclosure were houses and caves. An enclosed passageway, or "waterway," led to the nearby branch of Contentea Creek. When Colonel Moore arrived before this impressive fortification, he began careful preparations to destroy it. Three batteries were constructed nearby and from the Yamassee Battery facing the fort, a zig-zag trench was dug to within a few yards of the front wall. This trench provided protective cover for men to approach and build a blockhouse and battery near the fort. Both of these structures were higher than the walls of the fort so that the enemy within might be subjected to direct fire. A tunnel also extended from the trench to the front wall so that it might be undermined with explosives. On the morning of March 20th, every man was at his post when a trumpet sounded the signal for the attack. Three days later Fort Neoheroka lay a smouldering ruin and the enemy acknowledged defeat. The enemy loss was 950, about half killed and the balance taken into slavery. Moore's loss was fifty-seven killed and eighty-two wounded. With this one crushing blow, the power of the Tuscarora nation was broken.

Following their defeat, most of the enemy Tuscarora who escaped fled north to live among the Five Nations Confederation which afterwards became the Six Nations. Some thought was given to ridding the colony of all members of the tribe but was abandoned. For one thing, there was not sufficient food available to maintain the troops in service. Too, it was felt that some friendly natives on the frontier would protect the settlements against hostiles. For these reasons, a treaty of peace was finally concluded with King Blount and the upper Tuscarora. By the terms of this treaty, Blount was acknowledged chief of all the Tuscarora and of all other Indians south of the Pamlico River. All who accepted Blount's leadership became tributary Indians under the protection of the government of North Carolina and were assigned a reservation on the Pamlico River. All who rejected him were considered enemies of the government. These included only a small number of the hostile Tuscarora who remained in the colony and a few Coree and Matchapunga, or Mattamuskeet.

At first there were only about fifty of the hostiles, but they proved to be an elusive enemy. A few lurked about Core Sound, but the balance hid out in the Great Alligator Swamp, a vast and almost impenetrable region of lakes and cane swamps lying between the Matchapunga River and Roanoke Island. From this hiding place, they raided the outlying settlements. In the spring of 1713, twenty settlers on the Alligator River were killed. A short while later, twenty-five more met the same fate on Roanoke Island. Many others were killed in frequent and less dramatic raids involving no more than two or three families. After their attacks, the Indians retreated back into their swamp world where it was almost impossible to follow them. Colonel Moore, with more than a hundred of his Indians, remained in

North Carolina for some time in a futile effort to seize them. Blount and his Tuscarora finally came to the aid of the colonists and were more successful. By the autumn of 1713, they had brought in about thirty hostile scalps. However, other warriors joined the enemy from time to time. This nagging problem had dragged on for almost two years when the government finally turned from a policy of extermination of the hostiles to one of peaceful agreement. On February 11, 1715, a treaty of peace was made with the surviving hostiles and they were assigned a reservation on Lake Mattamuskeet in Hyde County. This was the final act of the Tuscarora War.

CHAPTER VI

The Yamassee and Cheraw Wars 1715-1718

The feeling of relief that came to the North Carolinians with the final ending of the Tuscarora War did not last long. Only a few weeks later the peace of the colony was again threatened by the outbreak of the Yamassee War in South Carolina.

The Yamassee War conspiracy apparently originated with the powerful Creek, or Muskogee, Confederation of what is now Georgia and Alabama. It also involved the Choctaw Indians, farther to the west, and all of the tribes of South Carolina. Below Charles Town, the most important hostiles were the Yamassee who had done such great service for North Carolina in its recent troubles. Above Charles Town the Catawba, Cheraw, Cape Fear and Waccamaw were among the Siouan tribes that also turned on the whites. The Cherokee of the west were involved to a lesser extent.

Concern over land motivated some of the tribes nearest the white settlements, but the primary cause of the Yamassee War was unfair trading practices and abuse of the Indians by the traders. The first blow was struck on Good Friday, April 15, 1715, when the Yamassee killed a number of white traders in one of their towns. Traders also were killed among the Creek and other tribes. The Yamassee and their allies swept across the southern frontier of South Carolina, leaving death and destruction in their path. The danger drew closer and closer to Charles Town. An expedition of colonists marched into the Indian country and dealt a serious blow to the Yamassee by killing a number of their leaders in battle. This blow calmed the Yamassee for awhile and the

colony hurriedly turned to preparations for its defense.
Three regiments were raised under James Moore, now a lieu-
tenant-general, and a chain of fortified garrisons were built
around the plantation country surrounding Charles Town.
In the meantime appeals for help had gone out to North
Carolina and other English colonies.

By early June, the southern frontier was quiet when
violence shook the northern frontier along the Santee River.
An Indian war party attacked plantations and captured
the protecting garrison, the northernmost of the defensive
posts. Many whites were killed and the others fled to Charles
Town. The Santee frontier was deserted. Except for about
seventy Cherokee, the Indian party was made up of various
Siouan tribes of east Carolina. The most hostile and destructive of these were the Cheraw of the Pee Dee River.

A few days later a detachment of troops went out from
Charles Town against the raiders and a number of the
Indians were killed and others captured. Those that escaped,
particularly the Cheraw, continued to be a menace. As a consequence, Charles Craven, Governor of South Carolina, made
plans for South Carolina troops to join others from North
Carolina in an expedition against the Cheraw.

North Carolina had already organized two volunteer companies to aid South Carolina. One company under Colonel
Theophelus Hastings was to go by water and the other,
under Colonel Maurice Moore, was to march overland to
join Governor Craven. Both Moore and Hastings were former
South Carolinians who had gone to North Carolina to aid
in the fight against the Tuscarora and who had remained
to make their homes.

By mid-July, 1715, Craven, feeling that Charles Town
was secure, moved out of the city with 700 men to meet
Maurice Moore and his company which included whites

along with a number of Tuscarora and Coree warriors.
Moore's line of march took him by Cape Fear but before
arriving there he learned the Cape Fear Indians and the
nearby Waccamaw tribe of the Waccamaw River, planned
to ambush him. Because of his advance information, he was
able not only to avoid the ambush but also to strike a
devastating blow against the two tribes. He marched into
their towns and seized arms and ammunition which they
apparently were receiving from the Cheraw. He also took a
number of prisoners but was unable to take more than
eighty or so along with him.

Moore continued his march southward but, in the meantime, the expedition against the Cheraw had been abandoned. Craven had reached the Santee when he learned that
Charles Town was again endangered by Indians from the
south, and he turned back to aid in its defense. Moore continued on to St. Julien's Plantation at the head of the Cooper
River, to await further orders.

In the autumn of 1715, after the harvests were in and food
was plentiful, offensive operations against the Indians were
resumed. News came in that the Yamassee had moved below
the Savannah River. Troops sent against them found they had
moved on southward into Spanish Florida. An expedition
was planned against the Creek also. They had confined their
activity in the war to killing English traders, but they remained the greatest danger. It was hoped the conflict could
be ended with a decisive victory over them. The Cherokee,
even though some of their warriors had taken part in the
Santee raids, promised to join in the attack against the
Creek, their ancient enemies. In November, 1715, the South
Carolina troops gathered at the agreed meeting place but
the Cherokee did not appear. Their failure to do so caused
grave concern. It also raised a question. Would the Cherokee

join the Creek, or could they be persuaded to help the whites? The salvation of the colony depended upon the answer to this question. Maurice Moore was sent to the Cherokee to learn the answer.

Near the end of 1715, Maurice Moore marched westward into the Cherokee country at the head of 300 men. With him were Colonel Theophelus Hastings and his North Carolina company. The size of Moore's force no doubt impressed the Cherokee, but his skill at Indian diplomacy was his strongest weapon and was the reason for the success of his mission. Creek agents were already among the Cherokee, attempting to persuade them to join in the war against the whites. The answer of the Cherokee was to kill the Creek visitors and to pledge support to South Carolina.

Maurice Moore's mission to the Cherokee was the most important single accomplishment of the Yamassee War. He won the Cherokee to the English at a time they might have turned against them. The union of the Cherokee and the Creek could have been disastrous. The salvation of South Carolina, and perhaps much of English America, was due to Maurice Moore's powers of persuasion.

Leaving Hastings and his company among the Cherokee, Moore returned to Charles Town in the spring of 1716 and later continued on to North Carolina. The end of the Yamassee War soon followed, though occasional raids took place for some time. The Yamassee were already in Florida and the easternmost Creek moved farther west away from the white settlements. A treaty with them was completed the following year. The Catawba and lesser Siouan tribes followed the example of the Cherokee and made peace. Only the Cheraw remained hostile and they became a problem of North Carolina.

While the potential danger to North Carolina had been great, the Yamassee War had little direct effect in that area. At the outbreak, a patrol was established between the Neuse and Pamlico Rivers. In addition, efforts were made to prevent inhabitants from fleeing the colony and weakening it as had been done in the Tuscarora War. In June, 1715, "strange" Indians were reported on the upper Neuse, occupying the fortifications abandoned by the enemy Tuscarora after their defeat. Unwisely, the colonists had not destroyed the structures. These Indians were probably the Cheraw and their allies who fled northward after their defeat on the Santee River. A military company of colonists and friendly Indians was sent out to investigate, but the danger was not ended. Raids were made against the local natives and a number of Cape Fear Indians were killed before they joined in the war against the whites. A wave of fear swept over the settlers that they too would be attacked. A small white settlement on the Cape Fear River was destroyed. The destruction might have been the work of the "strange" Indians, or it might have been done by the same Cape Fear and Waccamaw warriors who planned to ambush Maurice Moore and his company. In either case, another attempt of the whites to occupy the Cape Fear country was ended by Indian violence. In the autumn of 1715, the Coree, and probably the Matchapunga also, took up arms but were again at peace by the following spring. The principal threat to the colony continued to be the Cheraw.

Soon after their defeat at the Santee River, the Cheraw sought to make peace with the South Carolina government through Governor Spotswood of Virginia. Because South Carolina officials resented Spotswood's interference, the peace offer was refused. Soon afterwards, the Cheraw escaped a possible crushing defeat when, as we have seen, Craven's expedition against them was abandoned.

Spotswood's interest in the Cheraw and in their trade continued, and in August, 1716, he requested the North Carolina government to allow them to settle, along with two other small bodies of Indians, at Eno Town, on the upper Neuse River. There were about 500 of the Indians. Because of the nearness to the white settlements and because of their hostile nature, the request was refused. North Carolina, instead, declared war on the Cheraw. Part, or all, of that tribe were already on the North Carolina frontier and a military unit of whites and friendly Indians was sent out to attack them. The Cheraw were found to be well armed, and it was suspected they were receiving the guns and ammunition from Virginia traders. The Virginia government was asked to end such trade until the tribe had made peace with both North and South Carolina. An appeal was also made to Virginia for aid in the Cheraw War, but the appeal was denied.

In the spring of 1717, the Cheraw once more requested peace with South Carolina, but their peace offering was considered insufficient and was refused. As a result, they continued on the upper Neuse. Living in constant fear of attack by these Indians, the Tuscarora asked that they be moved from their land on the Pamlico to a more secure reservation on the Roanoke River. The request was made to the North Carolina government and was granted.

In the summer of 1718, the Cheraw were still on the frontier and appeared to have been joined by northern Indians as well as a few local natives. The government finally took more decisive action to protect the colonists and to destroy the enemy. Four companies were organized, each containing ten white men and ten Indians. One company was stationed at the forks of the Neuse above Fort Barnwell and the other at Core Sound. A company was also assigned to patrol each side of the Neuse. The continued service of these companies was considered necessary as late as November, 1718, but the Indian danger passed soon after that. The North Carolina government had already turned its attention to the more pressing problem of pirates such as Blackbeard. The Cheraw soon moved westward and settled near the Catawba.

CHAPTER VII

The Decline of the Coastal Plain Indians; 1718-1750

The long years of Indian warfare left North Carolina in a depressed condition. Property had been destroyed and trade had almost ceased. Poverty was widespread. Many of its inhabitants had been killed and others had left to seek homes elsewhere. There was little to encourage new settlers to come in. As time passed, though, the colony slowly recovered. In 1726, with the Indian danger past, the whites finally succeeded in establishing a permanent settlement on the Cape Fear River. With this settlement, North Carolina gained its first deep-water seaport and the trade of the colony was stimulated. Better administration came in 1729 when the British Crown took over the direct operation of the government from the Lords Proprietors and North Carolina became a royal colony.

At the time, white settlement was still confined to the Coastal Plain and within that area only six Indian tribes remained, or had retained their tribal identity: the Hatteras, Matchapunga, Poteskeet, Chowanoc, Meherrin and Tuscarora. Each group occupied an assigned reservation within the area of white settlement. Of the six, only one, the Tuscarora with 200 warriors and about 600 people, had as many as twenty families. Members of some of the smaller tribes had combined with the existing groups. The Cape Fears, already tributary Indians of South Carolina, were moved to that colony following the Yamassee War, or within a few years thereafter. Their power already broken by Colonel Maurice Moore in 1715, they were soon facing extinction by Seneca warriors. In January, 1727, the remnants of the tribe were on "Mr. Nicholl's Plantation" in South Carolina, awaiting removal to a more secure home farther south.

The Woccon Indians, the Siouan tribe which Lawson placed a few miles to the south of the lower, or hostile, Tuscarora, ceased to exist by the name. During the Tuscarora War, two Woccon warriors were arrested in Virginia, charged only with leaving North Carolina without permission. No mention was made of others being there. Since the tribe numbered about 350 people, it is unlikely all could have gone there without attracting more notice. More probably, they moved as a group southward and became the Waccamaw Indians. Tribal names were often changed or altered, especially by the whites in their spelling, and the Waccamaw appear first in historical records at about the same time the Woccon disappeared. The first such mention of the Waccamaw, by that name, was in 1712 when a special effort was made to persuade them, along with the Cape Fears, to join James Moore's expedition against the Tuscarora.

The Tuscarora under Blount continued to live in peace with the people of North Carolina, but Blount was not always able to control his people. Incited by northern Indians who came into the colony, young Tuscarora warriors sometimes ventured into Virginia or South Carolina and abused the small tribes in those colonies. Protests were made by both governments, but the raids continued.

One particularly provoking raid into South Carolina in 1731 almost led to a major Indian war. Angered over the theft of property and the mistreatment of white settlers as well as local Indians, the governor of South Carolina sent an agent to the Tuscarora to demand payment for the property and a promise that the Tuscarora would never again enter South Carolina. The Indians admitted that several of their men had been with the raiding party but claimed that all the damage had been done by Seneca warriors. They agreed to remain out of South Carolina but refused to make payment even though George Burrington, then governor of North Carolina, urged them to do so. The South Carolina agent then threatened the Tuscarora with attack by the Cherokee and Catawba and, if necessary, by the people of South Carolina also. Burrington warned the Indians if war came, the people of North Carolina would support those of South Carolina. The Indians still refused to pay.

In the tense weeks that followed, the Tuscarora informed Burrington that the northern Iroquois had promised to send 1,000 warriors to their aid if war came, and that some of them had already arrived. The Tuscarora added that a major war against the English in general would be the result. Alarmed at the possibility of such a war, Burrington notified the government in England of the danger. The answer came in orders to both Burrington and the governor of South Carolina to do everything possible to avoid the conflict. Instructions also went to the governor of New York to use his influence to prevent the northern Iroquois from becoming involved. By the end of 1731, the danger had passed, but from it the Tuscarora had learned a lesson. Afterwards, they were content to live in peace, with only occasional and minor clashes with Catawba hunting parties. These conflicts were welcomed by the whites as a means of draining off aggressive tendencies that otherwise might be directed against them. In 1731, Governor Burrington reported, "Our affairs are in as good condition as can be desired in respect to the Indians in this and the neighboring governments." The Coastal Plain Indians of North Carolina never again threatened the peace.

With the fear of the Indians gone, the government of North Carolina turned to a more benevolent treatment of them, though the colonists were not always so friendly. The government's attitude was in keeping with instructions from the Crown to regain the friendship of the Indians for reasons of safety and to increase trade with them. In 1732, a Commission for Indian Trade was established to assure fair trading practices. Efforts were also made by the government to prevent settlers from taking the land of the Indians.

Perhaps the most serious remaining problem with the Indians was over hunting. Because of the damage to timber and the danger to other property involved in their practice of burning the woods, the natives were forbidden to hunt within the area of white settlements. The Indians resented this restriction, and the problem reached a climax in 1740 when many of them were threatening to leave North Carolina because of it. Their departure would have been a serious loss. Too weak to be a danger themselves, they still were a safeguard against invasion by outside Indians. This value was emphasized in 1740 when rumors reached North Carolina that the French in Canada and Louisiana, and the Spaniards in Florida, were making unusual efforts to turn the Indians against the English colonies. The loss of its friendly Indians would have exposed North Carolina to hostiles sent by these rival nations. A critical danger would result should the local natives, with their intimate knowledge of the country, join the hostiles. To encourage the North Carolina Indians to remain in peace, therefore, they were given greater freedom in hunting. The problem did not cease altogether, but the crisis passed.

In spite of the friendly attitude of the government, the people of the colony continued to look upon the Indians with contempt and to abuse them. Broken in strength and spirit, the natives gradually decreased in numbers. In 1755, the Indian population of eastern North Carolina was reported as two men and three women of the Chowanoc tribe, in Chowan County; seven or eight Meherrin warriors in Northampton County; 301 Tuscarora, including 100 warriors, in Bertie County and 28 Saponi farther to the west, in Granville County where they had recently moved from Virginia. There were also eight or ten Mattamuskeet Indians and the same number of unidentified natives on the coastal islands and sand banks. The total population reported was 365 people, or less. The pathetic condition to which several of these tribes had declined was expressed in the words of a visitor, the Moravian bishop, August Spangenberg. "The Chowanoc," he said, "are reduced to a few families. Their land has been taken away from them." Noting that the Meherrin had also decreased to "a mere handful," he added," It would seem that a curse were resting upon them and oppressing them." Of the Tuscarora, he said, "Those that have remained here are treated with great contempt, and will probably soon be entirely exterminated."

By the time of Bishop Spangenberg's visit, the focus of interest on North Carolina Indians had already shifted to the west with the movement of white settlers.

CHAPTER VIII

The Catawba Indians of the Piedmont Plateau

The lure of cheap, fertile land eventually drew settlers onto the Piedmont Plateau of North Carolina. The extent of this movement was indicated in 1750, when Anson County was created for the convenience of those already there. In the beginning, Anson County covered roughly the western half of present-day North Carolina. In 1753, the continued increase in population resulted in the upper part of Anson being made a separate county, called Rowan. At the time, the two counties had a combined population of about 3,000 persons. In the same year, Moravians under Bishop Spangenberg began moving down from Pennsylvania into North Carolina. Their village of Bethabara (near present-day Winston-Salem) and Salisbury, the county seat of Rowan, were at this time the westernmost towns in the colony. Most of the people were settled to the eastward. There were, however, a few scattered and more adventurous pioneers to be found farther to the westward along the Yadkin, Catawba and Broad Rivers. Among these outlying pioneers were farmers with their families carving homesteads out of the forest. There were also hunters and trappers who lived as primitively as the Indians.

Some of the Piedmont settlers came westward from the coast. Others came down through the interior from the north. Among them were persons from Virginia, Maryland, Pennsylvania, New Jersey and New England. Many were Scotch-Irish and Germans, hardy and courageous people who were well suited to the taming of a wild frontier. For these pioneers of the Piedmont, like the earlier settlers of the Coastal Plain, moved into a strange and endless forest. They also moved into a land of native Indians.

Each settler who came to the western frontier faced the problem of dealing with these Indians. In a way, Bishop Spangenberg spoke the concern of all as he considered the wisdom of founding the Moravian settlement on land he first selected and later abandoned at the foot of the Blue Ridge. It was a chill November day in 1752 and the Bishop was at this camp in the wilderness far up the South Catawba. In the dim light of his tent he bent over his diary and entered his thoughts:

Our lands lie in a region much frequented by the Catawbas and Cherokees, especially for hunting. The Senecas, too, come here almost every year, especially when they are at war with the Catawbas. The Indians in North Carolina behave quite differently from those in Pennsylvania. There no one fears an Indian, unless indeed he is drunk. Here the whites must needs fear them . . .

Every man living alone is in this danger, here in the forest. North Carolina has been at war with the Indians, and they have been defeated and have lost their lands. So not only the tribes that were directly concerned, but all the Indians are resentful and take every opportunity to show it. Indeed they have not only killed the cattle of the whites, but have murdered the settlers themselves when they had a chance.

It was the misfortune of the Piedmont pioneer thus to bear a burden of hate developed in the Indian during a century of abuse. It was their good fortune, however, that the Catawba Nation, the only important tribe on the Piedmont Plateau, welcomed them in peace if not with affection.

The Catawba Indians came into what is now North Carolina at some unknown time in the past and occupied land on

the Catawba River, near its forks. The tribe was the largest
eastern Siouan group. Soon after the settlement of North
Carolina it was said to have included about 1,500 warriors
and a total population of almost 5,000 persons. John Lawson
visited their country in 1701 and reported several thousands
of them living in many towns. In 1738, a smallpox epidemic
killed many of the tribe and by the time the tide of white
settlement reached them they had decreased to about 250-300
warriors. The total population at the time was probably no
more than 1,000 persons, including the remnants of the
Cheraw and other small Siouan tribes of eastern Carolina.
They then lived in six towns, all located within an area of
a few miles.

The Catawba Indians were ruled by an elected "king"
and under him were lesser chiefs, including the headman of
the various towns. In making decisions these lesser leaders
had a voice in the councils, but the power of the king was
almost absolute. This made possible more immediate decisions and action in time of danger. An added source of
strength was the nearness of the towns to one another. The
entire fighting force of the tribe could be brought together
within two hours.

The Catawba needed all the power they could muster
because they had many enemies. Among these enemies were
the Tuscarora and the Cherokee. After their war with the
colonists, the North Carolina Tuscarora were too weak to
be a major problem and the Cherokee were too strong for
the Catawba to challenge in open war. The most persistent
and destructive enemies were the Shawnee and warriors of
the Six Nations. The Catawba were reputed to be among
the finest of Indian fighters and their scalps were regarded
as exceptional prizes among foes who came from as far away
as the Great Lakes to collect them. As a result, they were

frequently forced to defend themselves from invasion. They retaliated, though, by raiding the enemy country. The result was almost constant warfare.

Except for the brief period of hostility during the Yamassee War, the Catawba had always been friendly with the English and had traded with them long before the white settlers reached their country. However, North Carolina carried on little or no trade with the Catawba and made no effort to govern them; hence they became "South Carolina Indians" by becoming dependent on the trade of that colony. In time, however, the administration of the tribe did become a matter of dispute between the two colonies.

The dispute over the Catawba arose from the lack of an actual boundary line between the two Carolinas. For many years, while settlers were still confined to the coastal area, the Cape Fear River had been accepted as an unofficial boundary. In 1735, officials of both colonies agreed on a line that would include the Cape Fear in North Carolina and then extend westward along thirty-five degrees northern parallel, except that the line would bend northward, if necessary, to include the Catawba and the Cherokee in South Carolina.

This agreement, however, failed to settle the question. As white colonists moved into the west before the line had actually been marked, North Carolina officials became unwilling for the Catawba to be included in South Carolina. The continuing lack of a boundary led to disputes between the colonies over land grants to settlers. It also led to confusion on the part of the Catawba who tried to please both governments. In 1754, Governor James Glen of South Carolina instructed the Catawba not to allow whites to occupy land within thirty miles of their towns. This would have excluded almost 2,000,000 acres from European settlement, and North Carolina officials felt a smaller area would satisfy the needs of the tribe which they now sought to have included in North Carolina. They called in Haigler, King of the Catawba, and advised him to ignore Glen's order because the land belonged to North Carolina and not South Carolina. Haigler replied the land belonged to neither; it belonged to the Catawba and they would not give it up. The result was land disputes between the Indians and the whites of North Carolina who had already received grants within the area.

There were troubles other than land disputes that sometimes disturbed the relations of the Catawba and the whites. On occasions, the Indians robbed the settlers of food and other property. King Haigler excused the taking of food as a necessity of war when his warriors, engaged in frequent clashes with their enemies, had no time to hunt. The whites would not give, he said, so the warriors had to take. The King condemned the theft of things other than food and blamed such offenses on young men of the tribe who would not always listen to the advice of their elders. But even this guilt he placed, in part, on the whites who sold alcohol to the natives. The evil of intoxicating drink had become a serious problem to the Catawba tribe. In pleading with the whites to stop the sale of it to his people, Haigler explained that his young men "get very drunk with it. This is the Very Cause that they oftentimes Commit those Crimes that is offensive to You and us."

Fortunately, most of the troubles with the Catawba were minor ones. Members of the tribe guilty of occasional serious crimes were usually punished quickly and severely by their own people. Lesser crimes were not enough to break the peace that existed between the Indians and the settlers. This peace was important to both. The Catawba protected the whites against greater dangers on the frontier. The presence of the whites, on the other hand, provided some comfort to the Indians as long as the raids of the Northern Indians continued and the unfriendly Cherokee were not far away.

CHAPTER IX

The Cherokee Indians of the Western Mountains

The Cherokee Nation was located far to the west of the Catawba, in and near the Great Smokies. They were Iroquoian people who had moved down from the north long before the coming of the Europeans. The largest tribe in what is now the southeastern United States, the Cherokee population in 1729 has been estimated as 20,000 persons, including 6,000 warriors. Thereafter they decreased. In 1738, they suffered heavy losses from smallpox as did the Catawba. In 1755, the tribe was reported to contain about 2,600 warriors and a total population of about 8,500 persons.

The Cherokee Nation was divided into three sections, or Settlements. The Lower Cherokee lived in the eastern foothills of the mountains on the headwaters of the Savannah River. The Upper, or Overhills people lived to the west of the mountains on the headwaters of the Tennessee River. In between, in the valleys and the hills, lived the Middle Cherokee. Except for a few in Georgia, the Lower Cherokee were in South Carolina and the Middle and Overhills people were in North Carolina, including those in territory that has since become Tennessee.

The towns of the Cherokee were located on the banks of rivers and creeks, and amid flat, fertile land that was suitable for farming. Because of the rugged nature of the country such land was scattered and seldom occurred in large tracts. For this reason, the towns were limited in size, were numerous and were sometimes widely separated. In mid-Eighteenth Century, there were about forty towns with an average population of 200 or so persons stretching out over an area of about 150 miles. To the south of the Cherokee were the Creek Indians and far to the west, along the Mississippi, were the Chickasaw Indians. The Choctaw were located below the Chickasaw and to the west of the Creeks. In South Carolina, Long Canes Creek, about fifty miles to the southwest of the Lower towns, was regarded by the Cherokee as the boundary between them and the English settlements. In 1747, the natives had sold all their land claims to the east of that stream to the South Carolina government for the use of the whites. The unoccupied area between the Lower towns and Long Canes was part of the tribal hunting grounds and was considered not open to settlement. Because the whites were still far removed in North Carolina, no similar boundary existed in that colony.

The government of the Cherokee was somewhat complicated but was perhaps the loosest of all the Carolina tribes. Each town had its headman, but there were also numerous other lesser war and peace leaders. All were elected on the basis of ability and past achievements. The highest war rank was *Great Warrior;* followed in order by *Mankiller, Raven* and *Slave Catcher.* The principal peace titles were *Head Beloved Man, Beloved Man* and *Conjurer.* War women sometimes achieved rank as *Beloved Woman.* Rank, however, carried little real power and the authority of the leaders was no greater than their popularity and influence. This was true even of the principal chief of the Nation, usually identified by the English as *Emperor.* Under this system it was possible for persons of lesser rank to exercise more real power than did their superiors. The wisdom and respect of the elder chiefs were usually sufficient to result in orderly government, but this was not always so. Hotheaded and impulsive young warriors sometimes ignored the advice of their elders and took actions that endangered the whole group. The same lack of control also extended to the various towns and Settlements.

Each Settlement was independent of the others and so was each town. Councils were held to discuss problems but the decisions were not binding and did not control the conduct of individual towns and Settlements. This lack of coordination deprived the tribe of the strength that it might have had otherwise. At times, some unity was achieved through leaders whose influence reached beyond their own towns. The degree of this unity depended on the individual. A more forceful encouragement to co-operation came from common danger that occasionally threatened the people.

As with the Catawba Nation, and for the same reasons, North Carolina made no effort to exercise authority over the Cherokee even though most of them lived within her bounds. As a result, the Cherokee also became "South Carolina Indians," tied to that colony by trade. The trade was conducted by private individuals who transported English goods to the Cherokee and returned with furs and deer skins received in exchange. This was a profitable business, but, unfortunately, many of the traders were rough, uncouth persons who abused and cheated the natives in spite of South Carolina laws intended to prevent such treatment. The Cherokee had been on peaceful terms with the English since Maurice Moore's visit of 1716, but because of the conduct of the traders the friendship was not as strong as it might have been. To the South Carolina government, good relations with the Cherokee were more than a source of profits. An unfriendly Cherokee Nation could be a difficult, if not impossible, barrier to settlement in the land beyond the mountains which the English some day hoped to occupy.

This hope of expansion was opposed by the French and

the Cherokee were caught between the conflicting ambitions of the two European rivals.

Between the English settlements and the Mississippi, and extending from French Canada in the north to French Louisiana on the Gulf of Mexico, was a vast area that was desired by both the English and the French but settled by neither. To the English this area offered the possibility of future expansion westward. To the French it offered the possibility of connecting Canada and Louisiana. To both it promised rich profits in the fur trade. Except for the Choctaw land along the Mississippi, that part of the area which lay to the west of present-day South Carolina and Georgia was occupied by the Creek Indians who refused to ally with either the English or the French so that they might benefit from trade with both. As a result, competition between the two European rivals was most active in the upper part of the area that lay to the west of the Appalachian Mountains. Through this region the Ohio and the Tennessee Rivers flowed like two great water highways and were the natural routes over which settlers would some day pass. The Ohio originates at modern Pittsburgh and flows southwestward to the Mississippi. At the time, the area was claimed by Virginia and was dominated by the Shawnee Indians. The Tennessee originates in the mountains of present-day western North Carolina, in land then occupied by the Cherokee. It flows west and north to join the Ohio near the Mississippi. The nation that controlled their headwaters also controlled the streams and the land through which they flowed. Both nations sought this control through support of the natives. The English already held this support because they were nearer and could furnish more and cheaper trade goods. The French, however, worked hard to turn the loyalty of the natives to themselves.

In their efforts to win the Cherokee the French sometimes used gifts and promises of better trade. At other times, they were more forceful with threats and even attacks by their native allies. Their best chance in overcoming the English advantage of proximity, however, was in building a fort among the Cherokee. The use of such structures in extending influence among distant Indians was not new, and forts built for this purpose served a dual purpose. To the Indians they provided protection from their enemies, especially to the women and children when the men were away at war. To the Europeans they were more important as trading posts through which the Indians would become dependents and, consequently, allies. For obvious reasons, such posts could serve their purpose only among friendly natives.

In the past, the French and English both had used such forts with varying degrees of success. The French had built Fort Toulouse at the head of the Alabama River, among the Creek Indians in the hope of winning their loyalty. The Creeks remained neutral but doubtless the presence of the fort influenced that neutrality. Too, the French had won a minority following within the tribe. More important, it provided them with a base nearer than Mobile or New Orleans from which to work among the Cherokee.

Of the numerous French forts in the north, two, Frontenac and Niagara on Lake Ontario, made possible control of all the Great Lakes to the west and also provided access to the Ohio Valley and the South. The success of these two forts alone was reason enough for the French to hope that similar posts at the heads of the Ohio and Tennessee would assure them possession of the land to the west.

Among the English forts in the north, Oswego, also on Lake Ontario, was an important trading post that controlled much of the Indian trade of western New York. It also stood

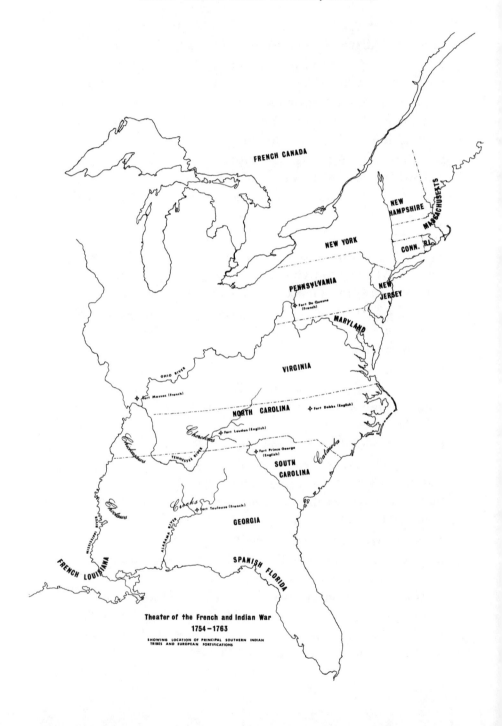

Theater of the French and Indian War
1754—1763

SHOWING LOCATION OF PRINCIPAL SOUTHERN INDIAN
TRIBES AND EUROPEAN FORTIFICATIONS

as a threat to the French forts, Frontenac and Niagara, and jeopardized French access to the west and south.

In 1753, South Carolina had built Fort Prince George among the Lower Cherokee to improve trade with them and to protect them against attacks by the Creeks. A similar fort had been promised to the Overhills people but had never been built. Neither had one been built by the French in spite of occasional rumors that they would do so. At the head of the Ohio, though, Virginia had been more aggressive. They had begun the construction of a fort there to assure their continued control of the river. In early 1754, it was seized by the French and completed as Fort Duquesne. This act was the beginning of the French and Indian War.

CHAPTER X

The French and Indian War

The French and Indian War began at the head of the Ohio, but it was a struggle between English and French colonists for possession of the vast area to the west of the mountains. By the spring of 1756, it had developed into a formal war between England and France in Europe, and other parts of the world, to determine which would remain a dominant colonial power. The colonies of the loser, including those in America, were to be the rewards of the victor.

In the beginning, the primary objective of the English in North America was to drive the French from Fort Duquesne. Since the area was claimed by Virginia the accomplishment of this objective was primarily the problem of that colony. Help came from England and from other colonies but even so, four years of poor leadership and failures passed before success came with the capture of Fort Duquesne in November, 1758. Two more years of fighting passed before the English won complete victory and took over all French possessions east of the Mississippi.

During the first four frustrating years of French successes, the Virginia frontier suffered the horrors of Indian warfare. North Carolina, however, was spared all but fleeting touches of this terror. This was fortunate, because she was ill-prepared to defend herself. The only military force in the colony was the militia, with a regiment in each county. By law every man, except slaves, between sixteen and sixty years of age was required to serve in time of emergency and without pay. The militia, however, was of little use, because it was poorly organized and was not adequately supplied with arms and ammunition. As a result, it was necessary from time to time during the war to raise companies of paid troops, known as "provincials." Such units were authorized by special laws for specific purposes and for stated periods of time. They were composed of North Carolina men and were led by North Carolina officers.

At the outbreak of the war, several coastal installations were manned to defend against an invasion that never came, but the western frontier was left exposed. The best defense there, it was believed, was to prevent the war from reaching the colony by defeating the enemy beyond its bounds. For this reason, North Carolina troops were sent to Virginia and even to New York to join in the fight against the French. Within the colony, guns and ammunition were sent to the frontier counties for the use of the needy there, but otherwise action was taken only when occasional threats to the peace demanded it. The first violence came in the autumn of 1754, when a band of Indians, believed to have been French allies, raided along the Broad River and killed sixteen settlers, and took ten others as captives. Because of the lack of other defenses, Arthur Dobbs, Governor of North Carolina, rushed a company under Captain Hugh Waddell to patrol the frontier as far west as the mountains.

Perhaps the greatest source of security to the North Carolina frontier was the presence of friendly Indians. The Catawba were the nearest to the white settlements and were the most helpful. On several occasions they proved the value of their nearness. For example, Catawba warriors went out after the hostiles guilty of the Broad River killings. They failed to catch the enemy but no doubt they prevented greater harm being done. The Cherokee were farther removed from the white settlements, but they were nevertheless a protection against invasion from the west.

As important as the Catawba and Cherokee were to North Carolina, their help was needed much more in Virginia where the Indian allies of the French, especially the Shawnee who had shifted their loyalty to the enemy, were ravaging the frontier almost at will. Virginia's governor, Robert Dinwiddie, had sought the aid of both tribes but without success. As "South Carolina Indians," the Catawba and the Cherokee were under the influence, if not the actual control, of Governor James Glen of South Carolina. Glen was not on friendly terms with Dinwiddie and did not approve of his conduct of the war in Virginia. In addition, Glen believed the safety of his own colony required the presence of the Indians, especially the Cherokee, in their own country as a safeguard against invasion from the west. The failure of an expedition under General James Braddock to take Fort Duquesne in July, 1755, was blamed by Dinwiddie on the absence of the Catawba and Cherokee who, as scouts, might have prevented the fatal ambush suffered by Braddock. The Virginia governor, in turn, held Glen responsible for the absence of the Indians.

At the time they might have been with Braddock in Virginia, many headmen and warriors of both tribes were meeting with Glen on the South Carolina frontier. To the Catawba, Glen reaffirmed their right to the land within thirty miles of their towns. To the Cherokee he promised arms and ammunition to protect themselves against the French, in return for their promise of continued loyalty to the English. He also renewed the promise of a South Carolina fort in the Overhills country. At the same time, the Cherokee surrendered to the English king sovereignty over all their land. Unlike the earlier conveyance of the land to the east of Long Canes Creek for "the use" of the whites, the conveyance of sovereignty transferred only the right to govern the area. Glen's purpose in acquiring this right was to strengthen the claim of the English to the disputed area beyond the mountains.

After Braddock's defeat, the Virginia frontier was even more exposed to the violence of the Indians. Terror seized the people and as one traveller observed, "A cold shuddering possessed every breast, and paleness covered nearly every face." The chill of this fear reached down into North Carolina but, fortunately, the violence did not. In Virginia, however, the help of the Cherokee and Catawba was needed more desperately than ever. Dinwiddie had reason to believe the continued failure of South Carolina to build a fort in the Overhills country was causing the Indians there to lose faith in the South Carolinians. He also feared that this loss of confidence might drive the Cherokee into the arms of the French. To hold the Cherokee to the English cause and also to obtain their help, Dinwiddie ignored Glen and arranged a meeting between his agents and headmen of the Cherokee on the Broad River in North Carolina in March, 1756. At this meeting the Cherokee promised to send a large number of warriors to help protect the Virginia frontier but only after the completion of an English fort to protect their women and children while the warriors were away at war. The Virginians agreed to help South Carolina build the fort already promised.

The assurance of continued Cherokee loyalty that seemed to come from this meeting was soon a matter of doubt. Even before the meeting, a large number of Cherokee warriors had gone to Virginia to take part in an attack on the Shawnee on the Ohio. The expedition ended in disaster when the food supply was lost while crossing a river and the men were reduced to eating their horses. Hungry and disappointed Cherokee warriors returned home across the

North Carolina frontier and wherever they passed they took food, clothing and horses from the white settlers. As they had at the time of the Broad River raid of 1754, many people gathered together in fortified houses or fled to the Moravian settlement. Angered, some of the men prepared to go out after the Indians but were restrained from doing so by Arthur Dobbs, Governor of North Carolina. Dobbs feared that private vengeance might result in a disastrous war with the Cherokee, and he believed the French had encouraged the Indians to act as they did with that purpose in mind. This suspicion was confirmed by King Haigler of the Catawba who revealed that the Cherokee had confided in him that they were considering an alliance with the French. By summer there was a rumor that the alliance had already been made.

Because of the danger of a French-Cherokee alliance and also because of the fear that the French Indians would extend their destructive raids southward from Virginia, steps were taken to protect the North Carolina frontier even though the Catawba again proved their loyalty by helping to recover much of the stolen property from the Cherokee. The North Carolina government promised to build a fort in the Catawba Nation to protect their women and children in order to encourage the warriors to continue their active support. The Moravians were forbidden to fight because of religious principles, but they did build a log palisade around their town of Bethabara for protection. As it had from the beginning of the war, the town continued to serve as a refuge for neighboring settlers. Many left their homes and went to Bethabara, and also to Salisbury, for safety. Others sought even greater security by leaving the frontier altogether.

The North Carolina government also contributed to the defense of the frontier by building a fort in the wilderness between the Third and Fourth Creeks of the South Yadkin, a short distance from where Statesville now stands and about forty miles southwest of Bethabara. The structure, named Fort Dobbs, was fifty-three feet by forty feet and was built of oak logs. As small as it was, it served as a garrison for the troops patrolling the frontier and also provided a refuge for the widely scattered settlers of the outer frontier in times of danger.

In the same summer of 1756, a group of Virginians arrived in the Overhills country to join South Carolinians in building the fort that had been promised for so long. When the South Carolinians did not arrive, the Virginians were persuaded to erect a separate fort on the Little Tennessee River about a mile above the Town of Chote. The fort, a log palisade slightly more than 100 feet square, was completed in early August. The Cherokee headmen were then asked to furnish the 400 warriors they had promised at the Broad River meeting. They were evasive, however, and only seven men and three women returned to Virginia with Major Andrew Lewis who had supervised the construction of the fort. Even more disturbing than the unkept promise was the growing anti-English feeling that was apparent among the Cherokee. Because of this feeling Virginia troops were not sent to occupy the fort and it was never active.

The hostility towards the English reflected, of course, an increasing friendliness for the French and no doubt this shift in sentiment resulted from the successes of the French in the early years of the war. It became most apparent soon after they captured Fort Oswego from the English and thereby gained undisputed access to the Ohio Valley. All the southern colonies, including North Carolina, now seemed in danger of enemy invasion, and the Cherokee wanted to avoid ties with the losing side. The pro-French feeling was

strongest in the Overhills Settlement which was most exposed to French influence and pressure. For a while it appeared that all the Overhills towns were united against the
English, but as time went by, it became clear that pro-French
sympathy was centered in only a few of the towns. Accordingly, in the fall of 1756, the South Carolinians finally began
the construction of a fort in the Overhills country, on the
Little Tennessee River near the town of Tomatley. Named
Fort Loudon, the structure was much larger and stronger than
the Virginia fort and was to play an important part in later
English-Cherokee relations. The fact that many of the natives welcomed the fort while some opposed it revealed the
disunity of the Indians. By the spring of 1757, however, it
appeared that the English supporters had won out and that
the danger of an alliance between the Cherokee and the
French had passed. In any event, Cherokee warriors went
to Virginia in the spring of 1757 and again the following
year.

In their willingness to fight for the defense of Virginia,
the Cherokee were not motivated by an affection for the
cause. George Washington, then colonel of the First Virginia
Regiment, reported that they "are mercenary; every service
of theirs must be purchased; and they are easily offended,
being thoroughly sensible of their importance." The
Cherokee did indeed understand the importance of their
services and they expected to be adequately paid for them,
as well as for the fact that they were required to neglect their
farming and hunting while away at war. When they failed
to receive what they thought was just, they returned home
in 1757 and again in 1758 without having contributed a great
deal in the struggle against the French.

The fact that the friendship of the Cherokee still could
not be taken for granted was shown in 1758 when the war-

riors who had gone to Virginia returned home. While passing through the Virginia frontier they took horses from the settlers. When the settlers used forceful means to recover their property, the result was the killing of both whites and Indians. North Carolina was spared this trouble, and much of the credit for this good fortune must be given to the Moravians. Hundreds of the natives going to and from Virginia in 1758 were fed as friendly allies at Bethabara and they responded to this hospitality by peaceful conduct. To the grateful Indians, Bethabara became known as "the Dutch fort where there are good People and much bread."

The feeling of the Cherokee, especially the young warriors, for the people of Virginia, however, was one of bitterness and a desire for revenge. They were restricted from seeking such revenge only by their elder leaders and, by Governor Glen of South Carolina. Glen warned them that war against the people of Virginia would mean the destruction of the Cherokee. On the other hand, for peaceful acceptance of their loss he promised "presents to the Relations of your People who have been slain sufficient to hide the bones of the dead Men and wipe away the tears from the eyes of their friends." In November, 1758, representatives of the tribe travelled to Charles Town and received the presents. A few days later the French abandoned Fort Duquesne as a large army of English and colonial troops approached. Peace it seemed had once more come to the southern frontier. For the people of the Carolinas, however, the worst was yet to come.

CHAPTER XI

The Cherokee War; The Beginning

Many persons hopefully believed the French abandonment of Fort Duquesne meant the end of violence of the southern frontier. They soon found they were wrong. Having lost control of the Ohio Valley the French increased their efforts to win the Tennessee Valley. They hoped to achieve this objective by turning the Cherokee against the English and finally succeeded in convincing the Indians the English planned to conquer them and take their land. The result was the Cherokee War. To the Indians this was a struggle for survival. According to the French, English forts in the Cherokee country would be followed by settlers who would deprive the Indians of ammunition. Rendered helpless, the Cherokee men would then be killed and the women and children enslaved.

At first, few of the tribe seemed alarmed at this warning, but as time passed more and more of them came to realize the danger of the continuing westward movement of the whites. In 1753, when Fort Prince George was built, the settlers still remained to the east of Long Canes Creek and there seemed little reason to fear the fort. But soon thereafter, whites were moving across Long Canes Creek onto Cherokee land. Probably some of the settlers were encouraged by the existence of the fort. Some no doubt chose to regard the Cherokee surrender of sovereignty over their land in 1755 as surrender of title to it. Whatever the reason, however, game became scarce with the occupation of the hunting grounds. The Indians found it more and more difficult to feed their families and to obtain the furs and skins they needed for trade.

This intrusion of the English, combined with the early war successes of the French, was the cause of the anti-English feeling that was so apparent among the Cherokee in late 1756. The Virginia and South Carolina forts were permitted to be built but the Cherokee, or at least part of them, were also considering an alliance with the French. This feeling was strongest in the Overhills Settlement and especially in the Town of Great Tellico. If the French had been able to provide the Cherokee with trade at the time, they doubtless could have won them over from the English. Representatives of Great Tellico were sent to the French in Louisiana and Canada to offer their support in return for trade, but because of the war Louisiana was practically without trade goods, and the Governor of Canada promised to supply the Cherokee only if they moved their people to the Ohio River. Unwilling to leave their ancestral land and realizing they were still dependent on the English, the Cherokee turned once more to a friendlier relationship with them. Resentment and fear of the intrusion onto their land did not end though, and many of the tribe continued to favor the French.

The unrest resulting from the Virginia killings in 1758 provided the French with another opportunity to turn the Cherokee against the English. In spite of Governor Glen's attempt to satisfy the tribe with gifts, many of the young warriors, especially among the Overhills towns, remained in a warlike mood. Easily aroused, they were incited to violence that eventually drew the whole tribe into a disastrous war. The French carried on their intrigue from Fort Toulouse and also from Fort Massac which had been built on the lower Ohio, near the mouth of the Tennessee River, even before Fort Duquesne was abandoned. As agents to work among the

Cherokee, they used friendly Creek Indians led by the Great Mortar.

Soon after the Virginia trouble, Creek warriors appeared among the Cherokee with taunts of cowardice for not seeking revenge against the English. They also brought promises of ammunition from the French at Fort Toulouse. The younger Cherokee became more restless and more difficult to control. In March, 1759, the Great Mortar arrived in the Overhills Settlement and violence soon followed. Late in April, about twenty-five warriors and several headmen of Settico went out from the town on a "hunting" expedition. After their departure, they divided into three separate parties and a few days later the real nature of their mission became known when they killed fifteen helpless settlers on the Catawba and Yadkin Rivers.

At the time, the North Carolina frontier was defenseless and this doubtless explains why it was chosen for the raid. The troops stationed at Fort Dobbs for patrol service had been transferred to Virginia the previous year to aid in the attack on Fort Duquesne. They were not returned and Fort Dobbs had, therefore, been abandoned ever since. The fort promised the Catawba Nation had been started but never completed. Under these conditions fear swept across the frontier. Many settlers fled to the Moravians at Bethabara "as though the enemy was at their heels." Others took refuge in Salisbury. Some barricaded themselves in their homes. None ventured out except at the risk of death. Catawba warriors went out after the hostile Cherokee but failed to overtake them. The Settico "hunters" returned home with the scalps of their victims.

To prevent further violence, Governor Dobbs transferred the only two companies of provincials then in service from the coastal forts to the frontier for patrol duty. Major Hugh

Waddell, the commander, was also authorized to call out the militia of Rowan, Anson and Orange Counties, but he did not consider this action necessary. The Lower and Middle Cherokee quickly denied any part in the raid and William Lyttleton, then Governor of South Carolina, calmed the warlike spirit of the Overhills people by demanding the surrender of the guilty tribesmen. The demand was made through Attakullakulla, the best friend among the Cherokee the English had, and to whom he was known as the Little Carpenter because of his talent for building houses. The fact that he could not meet this demand indicated the ineffective control of the Cherokee headmen. The people of Settico did apologize for their wrongdoing and also turned over the scalps of their victims to the commander of Fort Loudon. These were buried out of respect for the dead. Governor Lyttleton stopped all trade with Settico but otherwise seemed willing to let the matter rest for the sake of continued peace.

The French, however, were determined to keep the Cherokee aroused. Near the end of July, just as the crisis over the Catawba-Yadkin killings eased, pro-French Creeks appeared among the Lower Cherokee who were nearest to the white settlements and who suffered most from the occupation of their hunting grounds. The Creek proposed a joint war against the English and to encourage agreement they brought assurances from the French at Fort Toulouse that plentiful ammunition and other trade goods were then available there for the Cherokee. On the basis of this assurance, the Cherokee agreed to war. The commander of Fort Prince George learned of this secret pact and reported it to Governor Lyttleton. The commander of Fort Loudon also reported secret meetings in the Overhills towns of Great Tellico and Settico, probably held for the same purpose. Wohatchee, a headman of the Lower Cherokee, claiming to speak for the whole Nation, denied the plot and informed the Governor that the principal grievance of the Cherokee was the movement of whites into their land. If the settlers moved back across Long Canes Creek, he added, the grievance would end. Wohatchee asked Lyttleton to receive representatives of his people in Charles Town to discuss the complaint. Lyttleton agreed to a meeting but he also took certain precautionary steps, ordering the sale of ammunition to all Cherokee stopped.

News that their ammunition supply had been cut off reached the Cherokee in early September, 1759, and it came to them like the sound of doom. This, according to the French warning, was the final step in the English plan of conquest. The reaction of the Indians, as might be expected, centered around Fort Loudon and Fort Prince George. The Overhills people crowded to Fort Loudon and demanded ammunition. When their request was denied, the majority appeared uncertain as to what course to follow. A few were more forceful in their thinking and acted accordingly.

In the beginning, violence was confined to the people of Great Tellico and Settico, the centers of French sympathy. Their anger had been stirred to fury by a messenger just arrived from the French at Fort Toulouse. He reminded them of the death and slavery that the Cherokee could avert only by war against the English. To encourage them to begin the war, the French promised ammunition in return for three English scalps. Within a few days, a soldier at Fort Loudon, the trader at Chillowee and a pack horse man on the trail paid the price demanded. The fort was also cut off from the outside world and no one dared venture outside its walls. There was more French ammunition to be had for more English scalps. As time passed, other Over hills towns turned against the English. Among the Lower

Cherokee conditions were no better. Traders from all over the Nation fled to Fort Prince George for safety and, with angry Indians lurking about, anyone who left the post did so at the risk of his life. The Middle Cherokee were divided in their sympathy between the English and French, and since there was no fort in their Settlement there was less evidence of unrest among them.

In late September, Governor Lyttleton learned of the explosive conduct of the Cherokee and immediately began preparations to march against them. He also sent out calls for help to North Carolina and Virginia. While these preparations were underway a large number of representatives of the Lower Cherokee arrived in Charles Town for the meeting which Wohatchee had arranged. With them were several headmen of the Overhills people who came seeking ammunition. The Indians found the Governor no longer willing to meet with them in Charles Town. Instead, he was determined to march into the heart of the Indian country and restore order by peaceful means if possible, or by force if necessary.

Shortly thereafter, Lyttleton left Charles Town bound for Fort Prince George. With him was an army of more than 1,000 men, later enlarged to approximately 1,500. Also with him were the Cherokee headmen to whom he had pledged safety on their journey to and from Charles Town. However, on the march west he violated this pledge by placing the Indians under guard and imprisoning twenty-four of them upon arrival at Fort Prince George. According to Lyttleton, this was the number of English subjects who had been killed by the Cherokee since they had been given satisfaction for their people killed in Virginia. The prisoners were charged with no crime and their freedom was offered in return for the surrender of a like number of tribesmen responsible for the killings. The Little Carpenter tried to arrange the exchange but was able to deliver only three. By fleeing or otherwise, the balance of the guilty simply would not permit themselves to be taken. Unwilling to return to Charles Town without some show of success, Lyttleton, in late December, entered into a treaty with several of the Cherokee headmen, including the Little Carpenter. Under the terms of this treaty the twenty-one headmen still confined were to be held as hostages until the guilty parties were surrendered. The Cherokee pledged continued friendship and the English promised to resume full trade with the tribe.

Assuming that he had restored peaceful relations with the Cherokee Nation, Governor Lyttleton returned to Charles Town early in 1760 and disbanded his army. It was soon clear, though, that the tribe as a whole was not willing to accept the treaty. They neither understood nor accepted the imprisonment of their leaders. To them, the word "hostage" had no meaning. Confinement meant nothing more than slavery and in this case it was the result of the Governor's deceit and dishonor. They attempted to gain the release of the prisoners, first by request and then by force. When they failed they turned on the settlers and dozens were killed. Perhaps the most murderous raid of all was suffered by the people of Long Canes Creek. The situation became even more explosive with the killing of the commander of Fort Prince George. He foolishly allowed himself to be lured out of the fort, supposedly for a conference with an Overhills chief. Once outside the gate he was mortally wounded by concealed Indians. The enraged soldiers inside the fort retaliated by killing the hostages. With the death of the latter, the Cherokee had neither reason nor desire to restrain themselves. The whole Nation united in war against the English.

Since her military force had been disbanded after Lyttleton's expedition, South Carolina was no longer able to face the Cherokee alone. A renewed call for help went out to North Carolina and Virginia. More important, British regular troops, then concentrated in the north for the campaign against the French in Canada, were requested. While he waited for aid, Lyttleton did what he could to protect the South Carolina frontier, but it was not enough to defend the people against the vengence of the outraged Indians. At the same time, the horror of Indian warfare once more reached the North Carolina frontier.

The killing of the hostages at Fort Prince George took place in mid-February, 1760, and at the time the North Carolina frontier was again all but defenseless. The previous autumn, Governor Dobbs had raised a company of militia to join Lyttleton against the Cherokee. The men were from the militia units of the frontier counties of Anson, Rowan and Orange. By law they were not required to serve outside the province and, faced with the prospect of leaving their families exposed to danger, they refused to do so. The law was revised and a new company of volunteers was raised but too late to join the South Carolinians. Because peace was expected to follow Lyttleton's treaty, the men were released except for a small number who remained with Hugh Waddell to garrison Fort Dobbs. These few men were all that stood between the frontier people and the hostile Indians. Even the Catawba Nation could no longer be looked to for protection. The previous year, smallpox had hit the tribe and by the spring of 1760, less than a hundred warriors survived. These, with the balance of their people, lived on Pine Tree Creek in South Carolina and such services as they could give were offered to that colony.

On the night of February 27th, Fort Dobbs was attacked by a large number of Cherokee who fortunately were driven off without having done much damage. This was the beginning of a time of terror. In the weeks that followed, Indians roamed the countryside, especially the outlying settlements along the Yadkin, Catawba and Broad Rivers. Once more refugees fled to the nearest town. Others gathered in barricaded homes. The only real safety, though, was found by those who deserted the frontier, and within a few weeks at least half the people of Rowan County were said to have gone. Scalping parties came to the borders of Salisbury and Bethabara and from the latter village the smoke of their campfires could be seen as a constant reminder of danger. At night Indian spies crept up to the walls of Bethabara and only the frequent tolling of the church bell saved the town from attack. Several companies of militia were called into service to patrol the frontier. No doubt they prevented greater damage, but they did nothing to end the trouble. That could come only with the defeat of the Cherokee Nation.

Governor Lyttleton was determined to conquer the Cherokee and he devised a plan to accomplish this goal. According to the plan, the British regulars requested were to join with South Carolina troops and attack the Lower Cherokee. At the same time, North Carolina and Virginia troops were to join in an attack on the Overhills people and relieve Fort Loudon. Between the two forces the Cherokee were to be crushed.

CHAPTER XII

The Cherokee War; The End

On April 1, 1760, 1,200 British regulars arrived in Charles Town under the command of Colonel Archibald Montgomery. The addition of South Carolina troops and Indian scouts, including forty Catawba, increased the size of the force to about 1,700 men. At the head of this army Montgomery arrived among the Lower Cherokee towns on June 1st. His men marched the last sixty miles without sleep, caught the Indians by surprise and destroyed all their towns, including their granaries, orchards and cornfields. Between sixty and eighty natives were killed and forty captured. The balance fled for their lives to the woods and to the other Settlements. Montgomery lost only three or four killed and a few wounded. After his work of destruction he led his victorious but exhausted men on to Fort Prince George to rest.

Before continuing his campaign, Montgomery decided to offer the Cherokee an opportunity to end the war. An Indian messenger was sent to the Middle and Overhills Settlements and another to the Lower people to invite representatives to meet with him to discuss the terms of peace. The Overhills people were short of corn and those of the Middle Settlements were almost without ammunition. Both groups appeared to want peace but remembering the fate of the murdered hostages, they were afraid to place themselves at the mercy of the English. When none came to him, Montgomery made preparations to march against the Middle towns. He left Fort Prince George on June 24th, passed through Rabun Gap and continued on down the Little Tennessee River. He travelled through a wild country of dismal forests, rugged paths and narrow passes where the danger of ambush was always present. It was terrain over which wagons could not pass and so tents and all other equipment not absolutely essential was left behind. Food and other bulky baggage was carried by pack horses.

Montgomery's objective was Echoe, the nearest of the Middle Settlement towns. When he came within about five miles of his goal (and about eight miles of the present town of Franklin, North Carolina), he entered a valley covered with heavy undergrowth through which his men had to march. It was an ideal location for Indian style fighting and sensing the hidden danger that might lurk ahead, Montgomery sent a scouting party forward to investigate. As soon as the men entered the thicket, shots rang out from unseen foes and several of the scouts fell dead. Other troops quickly moved up and the battle had begun. The firing was heavy on both sides, but the English could only guess at the location of the enemy by the sounds of their guns and their war cries. These sounds, however, were sufficient to indicate that they were numerous and were determined.

Montgomery maneuvered his men in an effort to surround the enemy, but natives fell back and took possession of a nearby hill. The shooting continued, but each time the whites advanced the Indians faded back. When Montgomery realized that the natives had no intention of engaging him in pitched battle, he halted his advance and ordered his men to march into the Town of Echoe. The battle had lasted only an hour, and the English lost twenty men killed and seventy-six wounded. The Indians lost an estimated fifty men.

From the field of battle the whites went into the Town of Echoe and burned it. There, too, Montgomery determined his future course of action. Virginia and North Carolina had not executed their part of the campaign plan by simultaneously attacking the Overhills Settlement and relieving Fort

Loudon. His own army, Montgomery felt, could not reach the Overhills country, and he was not equipped to carry on the style of mobile fighting the Indians chose. His wounded was his biggest problem. They could not be carried forward in a continuing campaign, and he had no fortified place to shelter them. Neither could he spare a sufficient number of men to remain behind and protect them. The destruction of a few Indian villages seemed little compensation for the losses he could expect to suffer if he continued. His only choice was to return to Fort Prince George and this he did, arriving there in early July.

Montgomery remained at Fort Prince George for several weeks and then returned to Charles Town, leaving behind 200 men of the Royal Scots Battalion to help defend the frontier. His orders had been to strike an offensive blow against the Cherokee and then return to Canada where his services were needed. Believing that he had fulfilled his duty he soon sailed north amid protests and criticism. Some, including the Little Carpenter, thought he could have continued on into the Overhills Settlement and ended English opposition among the Cherokee. William Bull, who had succeeded Lyttleton as Governor of South Carolina, believed that Montgomery's inconclusive campaign and withdrawal left the colony in greater danger than ever. The confidence gained in standing up to the English would, he feared, lead the Cherokee to even greater violence than before.

Fear of renewed fighting spread across the Carolina frontier. There were alarms and reports of scattered killings, but the Indians were less active than had been expected. The Lower Cherokee had been rendered destitute. Within a few months they had rebuilt their towns, but they were lacking in food. The Middle Cherokee were still without adequate ammunition. In mid-August, Governor Bull learned that the two Settlements had held a joint meeting and had agreed on a desire for peace on the basis of mutual exchange of prisoners and the abandonment of Fort Prince George and Fort Loudon by the English. Whatever hope this report might have aroused in Bull faded a few days later when he received news that Fort Loudon had been surrendered to the Cherokee on August 8th.

After Montgomery's withdrawal, the Overhills Cherokee, with few exceptions, had shown less interest in peace than in seeking revenge against the English by the capture of Fort Loudon. Since the beginning of the war, the fort had been cut off from the outside world and without adequate food its garrison of almost 200 men had reached the point of starvation and despair. For this reason Captain Paul Demeré agreed to surrender the fort on condition that its occupants be escorted in safety to Virginia or to Fort Prince George. The day following the surrender, while enroute to Fort Prince George, the Indians turned on the whites, and when the shooting ended, had killed or mortally wounded thirty of them, including Captain Demeré. The survivors were held as captives. Captain Demeré and his companions were killed to provide satisfaction for the Cherokee hostages slaughtered at Fort Prince George. The deaths in excess of the number of hostages were not intended. After this act of vengeance and tribal honor, even the Overhills people showed little inclination to continued violence. In fact, it became increasingly clear that more and more members of the tribe desired peace.

The French had encouraged the Cherokee to go to war against the English by promises of plentiful trade goods, but they had not been able to keep the promise. For them, the intrigue was an act of desperation that came too late for more than a slight hope of success. Even this hope faded in

September, 1760, when Canada was surrendered to the English at Montreal. By that time, or soon thereafter, the Lower and Middle Cherokee were in great need of clothing and food. Near the end of the year, representatives of several towns in the two Settlements came to Fort Prince George and pleaded for their people:

> That they are tired of war; that they love the English, and want peace; that they cannot do without the English, and want traders with goods as usual to come among them; that the French are too far off, and cannot supply them; that therefore they have now none.

The following spring, the headmen of numerous towns came to Fort Prince George and requested peace, explaining that "they should be totally ruined were they prevented from planting this season." The Overhills people, because of their location beyond the mountains, had fared somewhat better in French trade, but even they became disillusioned with their new white allies. By the spring of 1761, they were receiving little more than ammunition and not enough of that. Most of them were reported as favoring peace and Oconostota, the Great Warrior of Chote who had been the principal leader in the war, expressed his willingness to leave the choice of war or peace up to the Little Carpenter, who had remained a friend to the English.

From the beginning of 1761, the South Carolina government took advantage of the need of the Cherokee and sent a large quantity of non-military goods to Fort Prince George to be exchanged for the many white captives held by the Indians. By the end of May, the freedom of 115 prisoners had been gained in this manner. At the same time, though, the South Carolinians prepared to strike a decisive blow against the Cherokee and dictate the terms of peace in the heart of their own country. Again the plan was for the British regulars to join the South Carolinians in attacking the Middle and Lower people while Virginia and North Carolina troops attacked the Overhills Settlement.

In early January, 1761, 1,200 British regulars arrived in Charles Town under Lieutenant Colonel James Grant who had served under Montgomery the previous year. He was joined by about the same number of South Carolinians and assorted Indian scouts, including twenty Catawba under King Haigler. After careful preparations, Grant and his army of more than 2,500 men arrived at Fort Prince George near the end of May. There, he was met by the Little Carpenter who pleaded for time to go to the Overhills towns and attempt to arrange for peace before the whites struck. Grant gave him little encouragement and continued with his plans to march against the Middle Settlement.

On June 7, 1761, Grant led his army out of Fort Prince George and proceeded along the same route followed by Montgomery the year before. Also like Montgomery, his army carried only the most essential equipment and supplies, and by forced marches he led it safely through two narrow and dangerous mountain passes. On the fourth day, June 10th, he finally met the enemy as the army moved down the Little Tennessee, with the river on one side and hill on the other. The location was only two miles from Montgomery's field of battle. Caught in a sharp though irregular crossfire from the hill and the opposite bank of the river, the whites were in a dangerous position. Not the least problem was an enemy that appeared, disappeared and reappeared at unexpected places. The battle began at eight in the morning and continued until eleven when the Indians broke and retreated. They were pursued but by early afternoon had disappeared for the last time and the battle was over. Fortunately for the English, the Indians were short of ammunition which explains the irregular nature of their fire during the battle as well as their retreat. Had they possessed a more adequate supply along with their strategic position the outcome might have been far bloodier, or even reversed. Grant's casualties included about ten killed and fifty wounded. The Cherokee losses were no more, and were probably less.

After the fighting ended, Grant led his army into the Town of Echoe which had been rebuilt and where he established a base of operations. Leaving his wounded there along with his supplies under the protection of a guard of 1,000 men, he proceeded through each of the fifteen Middle towns which he destroyed along with more than 1,400 acres of corn and other crops. The Indians sought safety in the recesses of the mountains and offered no further resistance. This work of destruction required almost a month and it was not until July 9th that Grant and his men arrived back at Fort Prince George.

North Carolina and Virginia disappointed Grant as they had Montgomery the year before by not attacking the Overhills Settlement. In 1760, several militia companies patrolled the North Carolina frontier which suffered some Indian violence, but the colony raised no troops to go against the Cherokee until after the Montgomery battle. They were raised then only because of fear that Creeks would join in the war against the English. The fear never became a reality, and the troops were disbanded in December.

Virginia's military activity in 1760 was also confined to defense. In 1761, a large body of Virginians was raised to march against the Overhills people, but Grant's campaign against the Middle Settlement had been completed before they arrived at Stalnaker's Plantation, a short distance from the Long Island of the Holston River (present-day Kingsport, Tennessee). There they remained and Colonel William

Byrd, their commanding officer, made no effort to lead them against the Cherokee. In October, about 400 North Carolinians and a few Tuscarora warriors joined the Virginians, by that time under the command of Lieutenant Colonel Adam Stephen who had succeeded Byrd. The combined forces moved on to the Long Island where, on November 17th, information was received that South Carolina had negotiated a preliminary treaty of peace with the Cherokee. The North Carolinians then returned home and were disbanded. The Virginians remained until the final treaty was signed and peace was assured. By their proximity, the forces of North Carolina and Virginia may have encouraged the Overhills leaders to enter into the peace agreement but otherwise both colonies played only a defensive role in the Cherokee War.

After returning from his destruction of the Middle towns, Grant waited at Fort Prince George for the Cherokee to come in to plead for peace. The Lower Cherokee were still in need and the Middle Cherokee were in even greater distress. There was little reason to fear that either group would continue the conflict. The Overhills people had not suffered invasion, but they had become disillusioned with the French who had failed to come to their aid, and they were tired of the war they knew they could not win. When they received an invitation from Grant to send representatives to discuss peace, they were receptive but the principal war leaders were afraid to go to the English. As a result, the Little Carpenter was authorized to negotiate peace for the entire Nation. Grant presented the Little Carpenter with a set of demands that had been furnished him by Governor Bull before he left Charles Town. With some revisions, a preliminary treaty was signed on September 23rd and the final and binding treaty was signed on December 17th. Though negotiated by the South Carolina government, the treaty was also made in the name of all the other English colonies, especially North Carolina and Virginia.

By the more important terms of the treaty, the Cherokee recognized the superiority of English arms; prisoners were to be exchanged; trade was to be restored and 40-Mile River (the distance from the Lower towns) was designated as the dividing line between the Cherokee and the English. No white was to settle or even hunt to the west of that stream and no Cherokee was to cross east of it for any purpose unless in the company of a white or with permission of the South Carolina government. The most important provision of all was the one that restored peace and ended the Cherokee War.

By the end of the war, England had already won the French and Indian War. However, the formal treaty closing the conflict (along with the Seven Years War, fought simultaneously in Europe and elsewhere) was not signed until February 10, 1763. Except for two small islands in the Gulf of St. Lawrence and the city and island of New Orleans, all North American French possessions east of the Mississippi were surrendered to the English. New Orleans and French territory west of the Mississippi were surrendered to Spain, her ally in the late months of the war. Spain, in turn, surrendered Florida to the English.

The English government realized that encroachment of English settlers on Indian hunting grounds had been the principal reason why the former native allies had turned against them in the recent war. It also realized that England's undisputed control of the area east of the Mississippi would create fear among the natives that such encroachment would continue. This belief was confirmed in May, 1763, when Indian warfare again broke out with Pontiac's Conspiracy.

Pontiac was an Ottawa chieftain who resented unfair treatment by English traders and who was convinced that the Indians could continue to hold their land only by war. The result was his plan for all the Indian tribes from the Great Lakes to the Gulf of Mexico to turn against the English. Pontiac was encouraged to begin his uprising by French traders who deceived him with false promises that a large French army would come to his aid. The help never arrived and the conflict collapsed the following year with the defeat of the Indians.

Fortunately, the southern Indians failed to join in the plot and the war was confined to the north of the Ohio River. In October, 1763, to assure the Indians they need not fear the loss of their land, the English government issued a proclamation forbidding grants west of the headwaters of all streams flowing into the Atlantic. This Proclamation Line, in effect, guaranteed to the Indians the continued possession of their lands to the west of the Appalachian Mountains.

The following month at Augusta, Georgia, representatives of the principal southern tribes, the Catawba, Cherokee, Creek, Choctaw and Chickasaw, met with the governors of Virginia, North Carolina, South Carolina and Georgia. The purpose of the meeting was to discuss various problems, especially those concerning land and trade. The result was a more substantial basis for understanding and continued peace.

CHAPTER XIII

The End of a Century

The year 1763 marked the end of the first century of permanent white settlement in North Carolina. At the beginning of the period, the area had been a wilderness occupied by native Indians who lived a simple way of life. By the end of the period, the area had become a land of white men with a more complicated civilization. During the course of the century, the Indians were ensnared by this civilization and had become a subjugated race, reduced in numbers to a fraction of their former population.

The dismal state of the Coastal Plain Indians at the beginning of the French and Indian War has already been related. At the end of the conflict, neither their numbers nor their condition had changed to any appreciable extent. One hundred Tuscarora warriors and twenty each of the Meherrin and Saponi tribes lived on or near the Roanoke River. Apparently all three tribes occupied the 10,000 acre reservation allotted to the Tuscarora and their combined population probably did not exceed 300 persons. Otherwise, there were only a few survivors of the smaller eastern tribes living among the white people on the coast of Hyde County.

The Catawba Indians fared little better than those of the Coastal Plain. The Catawba had been of great service in the defense of the North Carolina frontier but even so, possession of the land continued to be a source of friction between them and the people and government of North Carolina. The South Carolina government had guaranteed them possession of all land within thirty miles of their towns. The government of North Carolina refused to recognize this guarantee and granted land within the area. Resentment of this encroachment led the Indians to threaten the white settlers and even to drive some out. It also led them to refuse to allow the North Carolina government to complete the fort it had promised to them in 1756 and which was under construction in the Nation.

During the smallpox epidemic of 1759-1760, the surviving Catawba deserted their towns and moved farther down the Catawba River to make their temporary home. As the epidemic subsided, they desired to return to their own country but with their tribal strength reduced to no more than 100 warriors in a total population of about 250 persons, they also considered moving westward to live among the Creek Indians. The South Carolina government still considered the Catawba a source of protection for the frontier settlers and, in 1760, sought to assure their continued presence and friendship by promising to build a fort for their protection within their Nation. The Catawba accepted the offer and in turn agreed to limit their claim to their old tribal lands to an area fifteen miles square. Their right to this reservation was confirmed by the Augusta Conference and it was also accepted by the North Carolina government.

The Catawba Indians continued to be bound to South Carolina by trade and to be recognized as "South Carolina Indians," but several years passed before a boundary line was run that definitely placed the reservation within that colony. Already an impotent fragment of a once powerful tribe, the Catawba Nation received a crippling blow in August, 1763, when King Haigler was ambushed and killed by invading Shawnee warriors. Haigler had been a great and influential leader and after his death the importance of the Catawba declined further.

In 1763, the Cherokee Nation was the only powerful Indian group remaining in North Carolina. After many years of peace, the Cherokee had fought the English and had bowed to them but had not been defeated by them in any real sense of the word. They emerged from the Cherokee War with little loss of strength. At the end of the conflict the total population was about 7,500. The 2,300 warriors included in this number were only 300 less than in 1755 and even this small decrease was due in part to smallpox and other causes. Even after the French were removed, it was rumored that the Cherokee would resume war. They were numerous enough to do so, but it was unlikely they would turn against the English, their only source of guns and ammunition.

The 40-Mile River was confirmed as the boundary between South Carolina and the Cherokee Nation at the Augusta Conference. Virginia also assured the tribe that no land grants would be made in that colony to the west of New River. There was no similar boundary established in North Carolina because the settlers were still too far removed to be a matter of concern to the Indians. With the coming of peace, though, North Carolinians resumed the march westward that had been halted at the beginning of hostilities. This movement was to add to the grief of the Cherokee in later years.

The decline of the North Carolina Indians from a free and proud people to one dependent on an alien race was a tragic episode in the advance of modern civilization. In the beginning, the Indians welcomed the whites as friends with whom they could share the land and from whom they could acquire marvelous new weapons and tools and such in exchange for furs and skins. To the whites, however, the Indians seemed little more than subhuman savages to be treated with contempt and abuse. While behavior was judged on the basis of the whites' own code of right and wrong, little effort was made to teach them that code. Their rights were recognized when they provided a profit in trade or otherwise served the interest of the Europeans. When they ceased to serve a useful purpose, their rights were ignored.

On occasions, when they realized the danger that faced them, the Indians fought to escape their awful fate. They lost the struggle because they waited too late and failed to combine their strength effectively against the common threat. It was not warfare with the whites, however, that brought about their downfall. Their decline in numbers was due less to European soldiers than to European disease and excessive use of European drink. Their subjugation was due less to military conquest than to dependence on an alien civilization over which they had no control. It was also a civilization of which, except for trade, they were not really a part—nor did they want to become a part. Their determination to maintain their native culture had already led them into conflict with the forces that threatened to destroy it. This same determination was to lead to further conflict and suffering in the future.